Searchin' for Psychedelica

C. Liegh McInnis

Psychedelic Literature/Jackson, Mississippi

Psychedelic Literature ®

203 Lynn Lane
Clinton, MS 39056
(601) 383-0024
psychedeliclit@bellsouth.net

Copyright © 1999, 2007 by C. Liegh McInnis for Psychedelic Literature. All Rights Reserved, including the right of reproduction in whole or in part in any form without permission in writing from the author.

LCCN: 99-070341
ISBN: (13 digit) 978-0-9655775-4-0
ISBN: (10 digit) 0-9655775-4-6

Other Works by C. Liegh McInnis
Matters of Reality: Body, Mind, and Soul (Poetry, 1997)
The Lyrics of Prince (Lyrical Criticism, 1997)
Scripts: Sketches and Tales of Urban MS (Fiction, 1998)
Confessions: Brainstormin' from Midnight 'til Dawn (Poetry, 1998)
Prose: Essays and Letters (Social Commentary, 1999)
Da Black Book of Linguistic Liberation (Poetry, 2002)
Poetic Discussions (Interviews, DVD 2005)
Introduction of a Blues Poet (Poetry, CD 2005)

Acknowledgements

To Monica Taylor-McInnis, my Wife (Soul of my Soul): How many tires have we patched or replaced on the highway to Psychedelica? Each one has brought us closer to each other, closer to Psychedelica, closer to God.

To my Family: The Foundation of my life. Thanks for the Love and the Food.

To Claudette McInnis (Momma): [i] love you.

To C. Liegh, Sr. (Pops): Thanks, man…

To David Brian Williams: My poetic mentor. Thanks for giving me a nest. Whatever it is, whatever we find…Mississippi will give it to us.

To Jolivette Anderson aka The Poet Warrior: Your spirit is my motivator. You are our Eshu.

To Derrick Johnson: You are a Civil Rights attorney in any day. We all need vision. Thanks for the eyes.

To Charlie Braxton: The Bridge. You are an anthology. Thanks for letting me read you.

To Dr. Jerry Ward: The Master. There is no Mississippi scene without you. Thanks for teaching us all.

To Dr. Hillery Knight: The Beautiful Poet. In your verse we find what God wants us to do…Love, enjoy, and celebrate each other.

To Dr. Marie O'Banner Jackson: For the one thousand time, thanks.

To Ezra Brown (EB): Mr. Jazzoetry. Thanks for laying it down every Thursday night. Your spirit moves us to greater levels.

To Tri-Tone (Rhonda R., Nellie M., and Rufus M.): We need you back. The students need a school.

To Terry Miller: Rainy nights and smooth horns…play brotha…

To Ahmos Zu-Bolton: Thanks for your life and your work. You are the eternal spring from which all poets flow.

To Kalamu ya Salaam: [i] promise not to talk when hip music is playing nor when masters are speaking.

To the JSU and Tougaloo Poets: Too Funky. [i]'m just glad that [i]'m here to watch y'all grow. Thanks for your dedication and sharing.

To Chris Burkette: Thanks for letting your home be our home.

To Sandy Smith-Vantz: Thanks for letting us hang at your place.

To Stan Branson: Thanks for the support. You are an angel to all Mississippi artists.

And to You: Psychedelica is a woman. Let her give birth to your Utopia. Peace, rain and sunshine…rainbows forever.

Table of Contents

Preface	7
Searchin' for Psychedelica	8
Creation	11
Definition	12
Love Is Life	13
Magic Pen	14
Ghetto Issues	15
Nasty (Three Way)	17
When You Ain't Got no Money	21
Choice…?	23
Dark Room Thoughts	25
Science	26
Brief Moments	28
Mississippi Like…	29
Manifestation	33
Premature: The Anti-Climax	35
Tangible Documentation	36
The Hug	37
Ghetto Psychedelica	39
Come On	40
Just a Thought of You	41
The Workout	42
Oh, How like God We Are?	44
Root Beer Floats and Chicken Wings	46
All Is never Lost	47
If	48
Psychedelic	50
Seasons I and II	52
Natural	56
Memory Child	58
Café-Chicken Grease Ass Nigga	59
Schizophrenic Tendencies	60
Poetry Affliction	62
When Was the Last Time You Were Properly Kissed?	64
Cool Ranch Doritos/Peanut Butter and Jelly	66
Letter to God	67
Something Strange	68

Thinking	69
Psychedelica	70
To Get Wild on the Nile	71
On the Eve of Suicide	72
For the Enlightened One	73
History Lesson	75
The Wait	78
[i] Will not Pimp Poetry	80
Until [i] See You Smile Again	82
You Still Stimulate my Nasty	83
Time Going	86
Life Is a Parade	88
Pre-Colonial	89
Psychedelic World	91
My Journey	93

Preface

What it is?—[i]'m glad you are not afraid to open new doors. Some people haven't recovered from the flu of my last confessions; some weren't infected at all. It's a lot more here since the last time, but for the first time [i] notice that there is still lots of space to be filled. [i]'m still trying to fill this hole in the center. [i]'ve spent much of my life trying to fill metaphysical gaps with physical pegs. So here [i] am, and here you are. [i] brought you here. [i] need an audience. [i] don't like to be nude alone. Who does?...Do you? However, you are much more than an audience. Your purpose is to help me complete reality's painting by supplying colors to my meaning. [i] need you.

Most of my life [i] thought that Psychedelica was a place. Now [i] know that Psychedelica is a woman. It's a brain in a womb. Some people try to find Her with artificial muses and plastic stimulation. This dries up their Nile Reservoir and Pierian Spring. You can get Her that way, but you won't know Her when you reach Her. She's inside each of us as the Sun is in everything. She's waiting on us to flick the switch so that She can fill us with the glow of the eternal. The Egyptians' Aton, the Roman Apollo, Constantine's Cross etched in the Sun, She is like Eshu with Her own surreal signifying monkeys, navigating us to that place in our souls that reconciles us to the beginning. For too many nights [i] couldn't see my way here for the fears and tears clouding my third eye. Now [i] know that was also part of Odysseus' journey, my journey along muddy waters to find the bank of wisdom. So, welcome to one poet's mind. Individuality is the yeast that allows us to recreate and create reality to fit our existence. History is androgynous because it is concrete enough to anchor us and liquid enough to fit our glass. Memory is always randomly selective like three card monte since it is the child of Experience and Perception. Imagination is the fertile ground of life, and Love is the swelling seed of humanity that expands as we evolve. Hate is a racist historian with no dreams who attempts to paint a rainbow with one color. How many hues are on your canvas?

Searchin' for Psychedelica

[i]'m Searchin' for Psychedelica, constantly settling for the delusion of ghetto fabulous oil paintings hoping to find the place where lions and lambs share their leisure time eating lima beans and drinking lemonade. But [i] can't find the Dawn 'cause [i] spend my time working from morning dark to night dark as heavy reading is checking my pay stubs and the second notices of my bills. Scholarly deduction, critical thinking, and problem solving are reduced to solving the reoccurring problem of paying a mountain worth of bills with a molehill worth of wages, forgetting that only Jesus can feed a family of four hundred with a two piece and a biscuit. Still, [i] need an award from the prize patrol 'cause like a magician [i] come up with a way to pull a fat rabbit from a thin hat. But, ain't no Nobel Prize for surviving poverty.

Poets are philosophers who aren't afraid to get paint under their nails, and [i] am a child of the orgy in my mind when Keats, Baraka, Prince, and Hendrix had a wang dang doodle all night long, causing me to think about "it" and how "it" and its "it-ness" can change the hue of my fabric, signifying the stone cold somethingness of our lives. With words [i] am a minor god (street corner wordsmith) ordering the universe, plucking from the stars what's significant enough to record in bound leaves. But, my edited, cut and paste, language and after-thought issues illuminate me as an invisible poet with an imaginary audience.
The light bill towers like a fanged Oak Tree
over the simple shrubbery of going to the moon.
Eating cheap pork today is a bird-in-the-hand necessity;
having a heart attack is tomorrow's arm-length afterthought.
Pragmatism is not a theory; it's a Religion for the defeated.
[i] don't know any stainless steel truth, any bullet-proof knowledge, or any capital (G) gods.
[i]'m hoping that all of my truths are interchangeable parts that fit the engine of any situation because all of my knowledge exist in the half read *Cliff Notes* of daily survival, and any other knowledge is excess, like the left-over parts from an assembly project that never seems to work properly, or like the student who proudly protests,
"If it ain't on the test don't teach it to me,"

never understanding that missing knowledge
is the missing link in the chain back to God.

Of course, all of my gods are
what help me make it through the night.

When Jesus fed the multitudes, we didn't take the lecture
notes. A hungry child doesn't do the happy dance 'bout no
isosceles triangle, and he ain't trying to conjugate no verbs
either. The thundering, belly-slicing growl of a deserted
stomach is avalanches and tidal waves more powerful than the
need to groove to subject-verb agreement or place poets into
proper time frames.
Morals are for those who can afford them,
and [i] have insufficient funds in my account.
[i]'m spiritually bankrupt.
That's why [i] take another hit, still looking for God,
hoping on smoke that my street corner prescription
will allow me to see His face.
My left brain and right brain are speaking
but haven't spoken to each other in years.
For art has been reduced to rolling a seven,
number of units sold, and who gets the panties.

Searchin' for God, settling for sex, can't see the Lamb's light
through the germination of cataracts created by the mucus
of day-to-day surviving covering my eyes.
Singing the hymn of C. Liegh,
which is often a serous supposition of suicide.
This is my revelation,
being another blues, [i] mean psalm, for David.
Still waiting on that sexual salvation, testify (mind if [i]?)
with my Cadillac and four bedroom crib, [i] think that
[i]'ve finally placed inner peace firmly in my front pocket
until the end of the month comes,
slicing a hole and pouring out my peace like running sand.
Then, once again, [i]'m praying,
sending letters from Hell post-marked by Armageddon
because my third eye has been poked out by the middle finger
of all the philosophy that [i]'ve memorized.

Now, [i]'m too philosophical for God, or am [i] just phil-lots-a-silly, measuring my evolution by how many toys [i] have? As literature falls on wax ears, stone hearts, and brains absent of minds, we are reduced to robotic beings with predictable software that crashes whenever we are forced to think; so holy that our ears bleed from profane language, but can turn a blind eye to a little black child drowning within a profane existence.

We no longer know God because
Nature has been cashed in for asphalt progress.
[i] needs to get high y'all, but Jesus don't come in a dime bag.
[i]'ve lost Heru's pager number, and [i] can't answer Ali's
call because [i]'ve got to go see the downtown devils and
do my degrading dance to earn my unemployment check.
And somewhere along the journey Confucius and Buddha
have been downsized and merged in the hostile take over
of my permed out, Westernized mind.
[i] need a hit of some pure, uncut knowledge,
but my fried chicken and pork infested psyche
can't take the real Funk (the one—the middle c)
of the universe. My brain needs an enema 'cause
it's constipated on capitalism. That's why [i] can't see God
when [i] look at you. In the cracked mirrors of my mind's
cloudy eye [i]'m a carnival show perversion, and anyone who
looks like me has to be standing on this stage of schizophrenia
right next to me. So, God couldn't possibly reflect like me,
couldn't possibly bleed for me. So instead of repairing the
old rusted pipes, cracked inner walls, and clanging heater of
my decaying temple, [i] put another coat of paint on the
outside and lie to the mirror of my soul.

There is an invisible glass ceiling just above
Baldwin's Mountain, and from below we can hear
the echo of "Sonny's Blues" as it rattles in the
translucent iron box around my brain.
[i]'ll continue to be a slave in Plato's cave,
until [i] realize that utopia is bathing in the bright, Black
rainbow light of the spaces liberated by Lazarus' corpse.

By the way…what's in yo' joint?

Creation

…from the fertile milky matter of Black, it, a single-cell of
energy, pollinated with itself and became the forever after.
The flame of time began to burn deep into the viscera of its
soul, extending to touch each end of the soil rich spectrum,
one long horizontal line and one long vertical line of pyre.
Fire began to expand and contract
like walls of breathing water.
A ball of scarlet gold formed in the center
of the night covered canvas.
Day divorced from night, the rolling sphere of raging red
blazed a timeline trench as pieces of flame pierced
the Black underbelly of the night,
leaving flakes of light embedded into its skin.
From the recesses of its bowels, it spew out a matter
that dripped and dragged.
It was murky and wet, solid and rubber, dusty and clay, and
became the dwelling place of possibilities, the zoo of life.
It saw the light shimmering around the Black as the flames
flickered against the edges of its cool outer layers,
tanning, browning, bluing and greening its serene surfaces.
The swelling circle pumped like a healthy heart as Joy
welled up in it and exploded wet shadows across the
surface; fish and forestry were born.
And the entity that became God turned its Blackness
inward in a circular motion, flinging paint everywhere,
creating a universe, 'causing the glowing ball
to become a pumping aorta.
The longitude and latitude of the flame
bounced off the glimmering circle,
colliding onto the shifting surface,
penetrating into the water which lay in Earth's womb,
seeping deep within its bellybutton, reflecting upward,
causing other colors to be consummated, an orgy of
blue on top of green on top of brown on top of blue.
A portrait painted by a Metaphysical Michelangelo.

Psyche/Psychological/Psychedelica (Definition)

The mind is a womb,
waiting for deep penetration and rich fertilization.
The soul is a yam,
sweetened by the sugar of pure cane knowledge,
sautéed by the melted butter of the heart,
and baked by the oven of experience.

      At the apex of its ripeness when it's bursting with fresh juices, it becomes Psychedelica. The moment and point where the tangible and the potential converge as two stars swooshing in the sky, and the sublime is the smoke of understanding. (Too Funky) It's the ultimate orgasm. The Master's ejaculation of the Divine that is planted once we transcend the planes of Plato's cave reality. It's where the body, mind, and soul intertwine like ancient vines on the wall of possibility and become amalgamated soup so that we can see God (in the charity of man sharing his crops), hear God (in the fluttering of the butterfly wings or the cooing of newborns), and feel God (in the warmth of the sun upon our faces or from the tingle in our hearts from helping others). Then we finally know that the sign is in our constant evolution and that God's face is a rainbow mosaic that reflects each and everyone of us. God is the single-cell of each and everyone one of us, and we are His molecular structure. Close your eyes and know with the knowledge of your soul. Peace, rain, and sunshine… rainbows forever.

Love Is Life

To each life
is fish swimming in separate directions.
To each love
is snow flakes falling on separate spots.
No two planet-bound loves
branch or rotate in the same direction.
You can never compare a circle to a rectangle
or recapture one with another.
Even blood can be divided by types.
There is only one Love
that flows as an exact replica of each river,
and that's because His name is impregnated with power.

Live to love, and you will love to live.

"Well, you know my name is Simon,
and the things [i] draw come true…"

"Simon in the Land of Chalk Drawings"
from *Captain Kangaroo*

My Magic Pen

A single star against the night, again [i] sit and dream
bathing in the redemption of imagination's cream.
Stroking lines about my page, [i] Lego a world
to gentrify the one [i]'m in.
Ambiguous faces in the dark conform and perform for me, as
many times as [i] have building blocks in my mind.
[i] am the scientist of my universe,
the botanist and the zoologist ordering the organisms
of my mind through my magic ink-filled wand.
On the fertile soil of the pages, [i] grind out my fantasies
finding an infinite amount of juxtaposed positions
from the dictionary of literary masturbation.
[i], alone, am Adam's Father, creating mock reality.
Faces blur and become one all for me.
In my worlds only a circumscribed lexicon leads to sin,
but [i] can still write your name in the *Lamb's Book of Life*
by the power of conjuring chalk.
It's erect and full of ink sporadically exploding onto the page,
leaving the stains of my mind.
With every stroke, [i] ejaculate my soul
another moment of a writer's stimulated mind.
And my hands firmly caress, sliding across the keys,
typos indicate an overflow of ideas,
and scratch throughs the fear of you seeing my whole.
But alone with myself, [i] am Eshu,
creating fruits for me through my magic pen.

    The writer held it up to the readers and spoke, "This is my body. Eat and digest it so that you may taste my soul." And they ate of him and became full. From their eyes was removed the nebulous film of living, revealing the bare naked body of Truth. No one was defiled, and they made agape 'til the Dawn.

Ghetto Issues

[i] wanted to watch the space shuttle,
Discovery Challenger, do its thing,
but [i] couldn't because my cable is a tenant
that has been evicted from my premises,
and the rabbit ears on my thirteen inch
ain't good for nothing but hanging up clothes.
Besides, [i] had to go and put air in my back tire
so it wouldn't be flapjack flat in the morning, keeping
me from arriving to the concrete plantation on time.
After that [i] had to get to the pay phone that Superman
hadn't used in years to get an extension on my gas bill
so that [i]'d have enough fire to pay my light bill.
Yet, [i] would have still made it home in time
to see the landing, but like a mouse in a maze
[i] had to take the back roads home
because of the viper warrant from my ticket due
to my expired tag that hangs like an albatross.
[i] don't know how they expect me to bench press a $150.00 ticket when [i] can't carry the weight of a $71.00 tag, but it's all tied to a bottom feeder cycle of carnivorous capitalism with a buffet of bills and a swarm of greedy collectors as I am always bait for the business of big fish.
Anyway, once [i] arrive home, [i] must get to my cocoon to rise early and take my sunshine-filled step-butterfly to school. The concrete-hearted Creon administrators mandate that caterpillars living within a mile of the educational factory must walk, regardless of the temperament of the raging weather.
Yet, if she catches a cold the district has immunity
from paying her doctor bills.
So, [i] couldn't watch the morning report of Discovery
Challenger 'cause the Crossing Guard told me that she
just orchestrates traffic. Her pockets are not stuffed enough
to protect middle-school project children from the
drug landmines and ghetto-reapers looking for fresh
souls to harvest for their crops of forgotten children.
So, [i] take my shimmering step-butterfly to school
after [i]'ve checked the air level in my back tire.

And [i] would listen to the report on the radio,
but [i] must listen for that tea-kettle whistling sound
my car makes when it gets overheated,
pull over, and pour water into the greedy radiator.
[i] would get some anti-freeze, but why pay $6.00 a bottle
to water the streets and bleed my pockets as [i] drive along?
And [i]'ve got to take my wife to work 'cause the temp agency doesn't provide a golden parachute to avoid the piranha prices of downtown parking, which eat $30.00 a week, as she only harvests $160.00 a week while unemployment is a parking-free yield of $180.00. Even with the sliding scale of these sharecropper mathematics, it doesn't take a rocket scientist to calculate that welfare becomes a more appealing playground than the dungeon of the working poor. Therefore, [i] drop her off 'cause garage parking might as well be a country club to us.
By the time [i] make it to work,
the other horses are at full gallop so there is no time
for coffee, newspaper, or water-cooler chit-chat.
[i] go into work hitching up the mule in full stride.
And [i]'ve been meaning to go online and download
some pictures and information on the shuttle,
but my puny garden hose modem can't hold the weight
of water from the internet's fire-hydrant.
(The Smithsonian has offered to archive my system.)
So, [i]'m stuck with a computer that ain't nothing
but an overly dressed word processor decorated
with Pac Man and solitaire.
Oh besides, my phone is off anyway,
so [i] can't extend my water service;
thus, going online is a dried up option.

So, [i]'m sorry to report that
[i] haven't had the opportunity to put glowing eyes
on the spellbinding pictures and reports of the
space shuttle, Discovery Challenger.
But unlike NASA or the rest of the government,
[i]'ve been busy with my own star trek,
boldly going where no man wants to go,
being a husband and a daddy in the ghetto.

> "[i] want to multiply and
> do it to you from all sides…
> divide me baby"
>
> Prince 1986 Parade Tour

Nasty (Three Way)

If [i] could be one thing, if [i] could transform myself,
[i]'d be the keys on the piano. Then [i] could feel your
liquid essence every time you lay your fingers on me,
seeping your soul all over my ebony bone body,
playing your tune to which [i]'d gladly move.
Then we could make music
until the Earth stopped spinning.
Would this be Psychedelica?

Would that piece of a dream fit
into the puzzle of your mind?
Would you open to that idea
as a café opens for Saturday night bliss?
Would we need an audience,
a witness to incite, instigate, and induce our performance
to another sphere of the body's music,
someone to scream at just the right cue,
with just the right notes, hammering our harmony
into a well-shaped organ of exotic ecstasy?
Then the three of us could become one song.
So, as the conductor to our train,…tell me..
what do [i] need to do to carry home
the luggage that houses you two?
For every fantasy that you two could wish,
the three of us could be a human sandwich
of delectable desire satisfying sexual salvations
from the mundane Mondays of your mind.
If the bass of our hearts may thump, then
the three of us could surely hump
away anything that ills us?

Is that agreeable? Is that Psychedelica? Is that nasty?

Think about it:
three noses taking calculated whiffs of
each other's fragrantly floating scent,
three tongues flicking and licking
making tiny wet circles on tasty bodies,
three pairs of lips kissing secret parts
until rivers rage and break down dams.

Oh Damn, is that nasty?

Think about it:
Six arms and six legs, tangled and intertwined,
six hands and thirty fingers
reaching out for anything they can poke or find.

Is that agreeable? Is that Psychedelica? Is that nasty?

If you and your friend take me home,
the covers on your bed will smile forever
for we will be as snug as fitted sheets
on a throbbing mattress.
We could be three passengers,
each one can take turns driving this car,
then acceleration can freely explode through the curves,
over the hills, and deep into the terrain of soaked caves.
        "[i]'m a steamroller baby,
        [i]'m churning Earth into burning Funk."
[i] wanna feel two hearts pounding against mine.
[i] wanna kiss four pairs of lips.
[i] want the three of us to move as one body
stuck together like peanut butter to the roof or your mouth
with only my tongue being able to separate us.

Is that Psychedelica? Is that nasty?

Like a row boat in an angry sea, we move
up and down, in and out, over and under;
like a well-oiled yoga instructor, we
twist and turn, flex and flinch, inhale and exhale.

The three of us could make an isosceles triangle,
all three bodies converging into a prism,
an encyclopedia of sex
where the terms of who we are and what we can be
are continuously redefined like colors on a kaleidoscope.
Damn, Dionysius would be proud.
Is anybody in the mood for Caligula?

Is that agreeable? Is that Psychedelica? Is that nasty?

See, your stomach is like a slippery caramel snow
mountain where my tongue may go skiing
from your neck to your navel, tracing your treasure trail,
leading me down to your secret, sacred joy
where [i] may be baptized by the banks of your Nile river.

Then [i] turn, counter-clockwise onto my back
like the conductor of a three-ringed circus
to ensure that your friend is getting her fill.
Underneath the two of you [i] lay,
a butter-churned slave to your double wills
rotating like ice cream melting into milk
or heated chocolate becoming fudge,
until the three of us become one person
masturbating the night away.
Will Psychedelica be the steam in the midst of us?

Is this agreeable? Is this nasty?

Chocolate and cinnamon browns
swirl into a potpourri of pheromones and liquid bodies,
dripping with sweat and other assorted juices.
It's a cocktail of delicacies.
Combined, we are a tri-couple.
We'll try this, and we'll try that.
[i] pour both of you into a cup,
stir lightly 'til cream rises to the top.
[i] drink and become intoxicated.

Is that Psychedelica? Is that nasty?

[i] want to slither and slide through your legs
and snake across her thighs,
underneath you and on top of her,
you horizontal and her vertical.
We make one hell of an intersection.
My two busy hands and my eager tongue,
[i]'m a policeman directing this sex-a-pade.
You in front and her in back,
let's just say that [i]'m rubber-band flexible.
The truth is that [i] don't know but one position,
but [i] can do it eighty-seven different ways.

Is any or all of this Psychedelica?
Is any or all of this nasty?

Well, nastier is as nasty wants to be.
[i]'m just trying to see
if Psychedelica can be found
between us three.
Just one touch and a river begins to flow,
reaffirming what we all know.

All of this talk about social-political-humanity is simply
the urge to unlock the rising rivers of our nasty.

When You Ain't Got no Money

You ever notice that when you ain't got no money
everybody in your house is madder than
Jim Crow during Black History Month.
Everybody is segregated into a separate room
dreaming 'bout the waterfalls they want but can't get due to
having a pocket full of dust because the lake of your bank
account has dried from the heat of your bills.
Mad at the holes in your pockets from which King's Dream
has slipped through and crashed
into tiny pieces of Reaganomics.
Love is reduced to barren fertilizer 'cause it can't
fill a gas tank or put food on the table or pay no light bill.
When you broke love ain't nothing but
a remote control with no television.
And broke and angry fit together like milk and cereal.
You mad at yourself for not being able
to bring the buffalo home.
But you mad at your family for not being able
to hunt for themselves.
"Why can't twelve year olds work? They can eat."
And of course, they mad at yo' cracked and broke ass,
walking 'round the house like hidden landmines,
their eyes blaze at you like patriot missiles,
while they spew words of chemical warfare.
Yes, when you ain't got no money,
everybody in the house is madder than
Confederate rebels being captured by Black soldiers.

When you broke, you want to know why
your children need that dollar for lunch everyday.
[i] remember high-school food.
"Take this fifty cents and tell 'em you on the low cal plan.
You're young; your body
doesn't need daily nutrition, do you?"
When you broke your kids' college applications
are like lottery tickets that cost too much to play.
When you are broke, the only extracurricular activities
you can afford for your kids is the walk home from school.

We you are broke,
college is a compromise that continues the cycle of poverty.
When you are broke,
soft kisses are as rare as blue moons.
When you are broke,
laughter only blossoms on the first and the fifteenth.
When you are broke,
saying [i] love you is placed on a lay-away plan.
When you are broke,
your woman's eyes stab you with the knife
of her disappointment,
and everything she says sounds like noisy criticism
rattling around in your ears
like a rock pebble in an empty tin can,
making you feel like a marble eunuch.
When you are broke,
today is a magnanimous mountain
and tomorrow is a lump in the distance.
When you are broke,
the light bill is the air that you breathe and that
school sponsored field trip is an unnecessary fragrance.
Yes, when you ain't got no money,
everybody in the house is madder than the Klan
with the passage of the King Holiday.

Choice...?

My responsibility makes me first-response-able to me.
How you gon' strong-arm me to have a child [i] can't feed?
Two drinking from a budget for one will surely thirst three?
You say [i] should have read the whole contract—small
print and all—before [i] was knee-deep in the do.
Yeah, but abortion won't seem so bad
when my uninvited child is carjacking you.
You say that every child has a right to be born,
but you ain't trying to harvest extra taxes so that
each can be properly fertilized with a ripe education.
It ain't no secret; my mission was to get in it.
But getting condoms are like finding an honest politician
because your policy chained the doors to the free clinic.
And if you make us have this child that we don't want,
five will get you ten that
one of us will be painted dead or on death row.
Your number one song with a bullet screams
that abortion is homicide, possibly even genocide.
[i] say that for WIC and TNAF cemented Black folks
to keep having babies ain't nothing but Guyana suicide.
It's impossible to choose life
when you keep given birth to death.
'Cause if you think [i]'m gon' want the li'l crumb snatcher
just 'cause it's here, means that you still think that a fairy
gives you money for your missing teeth.
When she said she was pregnant,
all of my dreams became a raisin in the sun.
[i] should have thought about that before [i] got the panties.
But keeping my woman from having an abortion ain't the
magic potion that can abracadabra us into loving beings.
To be honest, [i]'m just gon' hate the kid because
its face will be a mirror of the moment that I died.
Now, for two minutes and thirty seconds
all my dreams are disco dead.
Maybe instead of getting the panties,
[i] should have settled for plan b: head.
But, one thing is as true as a spring rain.
In a bet of whether I'mma choose me or somebody else,

23

don't take the points 'cause I'mma choose myself.
So, dead or alive [i] won't love the child
whether it blossoms for a trimester or a while.
Your poetic photos of dismembered fetuses
are only a waste of film and trees.
True pain is a lifetime of being treated
like an old car in the backyard.
Then you say, "Well don't kill it; put it up for adoption."
Hell, the way y'all lumberjacking programs
that ain't a viable option.
Daily, you bitch about sprouting taxes
to take care of somebody else's child,
so you prune the funding to education
then bitch about my child being the weed in your garden?
You keep saying that abortion is a sin
until my thrown-away child boomerangs back
to rape your daughter and kill your son.
Then, I learn your deepest fires regarding abortion.
You have it stoked daily by the government
in its more mature form of blazing capital punishment.

Dark Room Thoughts

My head is throbbing like an incarcerated penis.
It's a swollen balloon with varicose veins.
Afraid to swallow another thought for fear
of circuit overload, and then my cheap calculator
will dump everything except my childhood.
(Last night, night before, twenty-four robbers at my door)
Can't afford extended memory for the laptop in my head.
My CPU doesn't have enough ram to process my life.
Afraid that in a desperate attempt to gain more space,
all of my hidden sins will be downloaded and come
exploding from my head like an overdue orgasm.
My past is a swifter sprinter that will spew itself all over
my now, covering me with the stench of who [i] really am.
Afraid to find that my future is just an ink stained
illusion of dusty delusions, my left eye jumping to the
erratic syncopation of my heart filled with icicle fear.
God doesn't hear the cries of a moldy mouth full of sin.
Redemption is a blueprinted process not a fairytale of
happenstance, and my brain has the wrong software
to run the program of atonement.
[i] can see the burning,
blackened chrism doors of Beelzebub's foyer.
Some smart ass has etched my name on the right door just
beneath Satan's. (That shit ain't funny.)
All my life my brain has had a blindfold around it,
and my soul's navigator has been perpetually intoxicated.
[i]'m truly third eye blind, bumping into life in the daytime.
[i] feel like a dick-less man in a whorehouse.
[i]'m standing on intellectual quicksand.
The more [i] think, the worse it gets.

Science...

Man's movement...
Spheres, spaces, things, and thinginess.
We need to open the back of the clock to see its parts
even if we don't know how to put it back together.
Though we know that Time is more than measurement,
we just don't have enough time to read between the lines.
Worlds turning, revolving, evolving...
spaces are given name tags and Nature
organized like a department store;
a light is shined. (Jupiter's other moon is found.)
Science, God's librarian to the physical,
gives us a card catalogue to mark where we stand.
Then we are able to find Wednesday in the middle of 168
hours as Science plots a course for man back to himself.

And yet, it is painful to lose my man in the moon,
the nymphs in my dreams, and
the angels who push the planets.
Now, who will paint the sky for me?
Who will tilt the world when it has fallen off its axis?
SCIENCE?...
It exterminates the myth from my history,
and the moral from my story
so [i] can now understand dead existence?
Now, with the cataracts of fable removed from my eyes
[i] can better see man:
understand his straw huts and his golden idol skyscrapers,
understand his turtle-slow schools and his rabbit-fast jails,
understand his vampire banks and its bloody money,
understand his barbed-wire system of separation from God,
understand his plastic peace produced by a gun barrel.
Then, [i] can see me in the mirror of man's mechanics.
[i]'m going to Pluto to get to Mercury.

This is Science, the great reveler
who pulls up the dress of Mystery
so that we can see her torn draws.
It maketh things smaller

so [i] can see them larger.
It places bodies in my hands
and worlds at my fingertips
to understand that the parts are the whole.
And in magnifying mankind's molecules,
making me see my own meaningless mortality,
[i] am drawn closer to God.

Brief Moments

Now and again, every turquoise moon or two,
[i] find a piece of Sublime lying in the rubble
of the discarded down here.
Briefly, in the order of random seasons, it plays peek-a-boo
as the outline of God's face flashes for seconds,
then quickly leaving me as late summer rainbows.
The residue of it lingers in my memory
like the smell of a long lost lover,
infecting my brain with what seems like
faint hope of a better tomorrow.

A revelation is a second-hand high.
An epiphany is some good weed where shapeless smoke
in the world of measured senses becomes
a crystal clear stairway.
The Sublime, like Time, overcomes us
like a Hurricane's flood waters, washing away
the locked gate that separates us
from the inside of Truth, and our segregated self
becomes, for a moment, one Nation under Peace.
Therein, Time stands still, shivering from the climax
vibrating its rippling waves through endless space
like the Egyptian hieroglyphics that still talk to us today.

It's a whisper, pimping us into continuing to evolve
by showing us the finished portrait while knowing
that we don't have enough colors to complete the painting.
Can man be God-like when he can't be Christ-like?
We are all hungry and dying from the fat
in our philosophies.
Searchin' for Psychedelica, finding brief moments
of the Sublime that is too big for our cup;
so, we drink what we can.

Mississippi Like…

What is it to be Mississippi?
Where Capitol Streets cross cotton fields and Margaret's
Jubilee jams with Eudora's Festival even when there are
college cuts, controversy, and the Klan, with plenty of
revolution, religion, red, ripe tomatoes, and
rebel's ruby racist rag; this is all my Mississippi.
It's little boys puttin' dirt in abandoned tires
then rolling the tires by little girls in their Sunday dresses.
It's hangin' out at Big Sam's Juke Joint on Saturday night
and jukin' to "Sign Me Up" on Sunday Morning.
It's pickin' wild berries and stealin' Mr. Wilson's plumbs.
It's mowin' everybody's yard 'cause yo' mama said so.
It's where time out means…
mama takin' a break from whippin' yo' leathery hide, and the
thought of a swarming strap still causes you to wake up in the
middle of the night in a cold sweat.
It's Ross Barnett damming the doorway of education
and James Meredith bulldozing over his ideology.
It's the Sovereignty Commission playing
hide-n-go-seek with the lives of invisible citizens
while Ebony voices declare "We Shall not Be Moved"
under the salacious sites of riffles and German Shepherds.
What is it to be Mississippi?
It's no matter how highbrow we get
we still have hot sauce on the table when we eat.
It's having a special jaw bone from being double-voiced,
being bi-legally lingual enough to talk with two tongues:
a democrat on tv and a dixiecrat under the hill—
wearing black suits in the day
and white sheets during the night.

It's cinnamon and coffee leaves hangin' from faded olive
trees, a warm Thanksgiving and a cool Christmas, where rain
steals center stage from snow, and a brief frost can close
school like the notion of the ending of segregation,
as Southern Apartheid is kept alive every Sunday morning.
We still don't pray together even though our children
can hopscotch over to Ole Miss and play together.
What is it to be Mississippi?
It's the peanut butter and jelly sandwich

of Archie Manning and Walter Payton
where some like peanut butter more than jelly.
Yet, half a sandwich rarely fills a whole belly.
It's the quiet confusion that becomes
too cantankerous to ignore—like when the doctor says
today is the day to stop eating pork.
Or, when the pork politics of "good ole boy" kick backs
become too fattening to nurture democracy.
What is it to be Mississippi?
It's having one street with two names so that
the white folks can live on Hanging Moss
and the Black folks can live on West Street
until the Black folks march up the street
'causin' the Confederates to retreat to Rankin County.
What is it to be Mississippi?
It's being the mirror of the world with a
Chrysler chrome reflection too bright to face.

Someone spat that to be Mississippi is to be dumb and stupid.
If that's being Mississippi, then [i] wanna wear the crown of
dumb and stupid:
dumb and stupid like Medgar Evers and Richard Wright
      who used the pen the carve evil into pieces,
dumb and stupid like Margaret Walker Alexander
      who used the paint of the past to illustrate
      new school prophets,
dumb and stupid like Etheridge Knight and Robin Roberts
      who weaved words into portraits of dignity,
dumb and stupid like Robert Johnson and B. B. King
      who took tears of bluespeople and made
      lemonade for the world,
dumb and stupid like Charlie Pride
      who put on white face with false camouflage
      to melt the plastic illusions of pale listeners,
dumb and stupid like Tennessee Williams and Eudora Welty
      two silver knights who believed that souls could be
      saved with secular bibles laced with gospels of the
      South,
dumb and stupid like Elvis Presley
      who took the juke joint of the ebony Delta to pallid
      patrons, liberating them one hip thrust at a time,
dumb and stupid like Bennie Thompson and Aaron Henry

       who sculpted voter registration cards
       into weapons of liberty,
dumb and stupid like Charles Tisdale and Mike Espy
       who wielded language like lumberjacks
       decimating a forest of fools,
dumb and stupid like Jake Ayers and Hollis Watkins
       who used the stallion of truth to stampede
       centuries of concrete lies,
dumb and stupid like Bob Moses and Alvin Chambliss
       who combined the artistry of agitation
       with the sword of litigation,
dumb and stupid like Gene "Jughead" Young and my father
       who paid my college tuition with jail-time currency,
dumb and stupid like Fannie Lou Hamer and J. R. Lynch
       who taught that freedom is the only medicine
       for oppression,
dumb and stupid like Henry Kirksy and Roy McCory
       who wore intelligence like a finely tailored suit,
dumb and stupid like Dr. John A. Peoples
       who with a gardener's love cultivated JSC into JSU,
       creating Mighty Magnolias of Mississippi's Modern
       HBCU.

So, to be Mississippi is knowing that decency, courage, and
forgiveness are not a three-piece suit that can be removed
when they are no longer fashionable.
Like, when you say yes ma'am and no ma'am because
manners are the concrete foundation of civilization,
that's the Mississippi in ya'.
When you open the door for a woman,
not as a prelude to a rendezvous,
but because women are the fertile soil of our futures,
that's the Mississippi in ya'.
When a family reunion is a Sunday dinner,
that's the Mississippi in ya'.
Or, when you send a plate over to Ms. Mary's house 'cause
all of her children took the exodus train North,
and she can't navigate the stairs like she used to,
that's the Mississippi in ya'.
When you go to school because education is the sledge
hammer to knock holes in the walls of injustice and
oppression, that's the Mississippi in ya'.

When you vote, even though there are two flap-jack
politicians on both sides of the ballot, and the concept of
Statesman is nothing more than a mascot for Delta State,
yet you pull the lever anyway because Medgar's blood
is the only registration card you need,
that's the Mississippi in ya'.
When being baptized in the blood refers to the plasma of
Jesus and the crimson of the Civil Rights Movement,
that's the Mississippi in ya'.
When you speak to people whom you don't know
as you pass them on the streets, that's the Mississippi in ya'.
And then after speakin' you ask them,
"Who yo' folks baby?" That's the Mississippi in ya'.
Or, when you see a stranger with a familiar face and ask him
if he's Ms. Ruthie Mae Johnson's boy,
who lives over the tracks, under the hill,
that had that daughter who married that Williams boy
whose family owns the stow next to the Saw Mill Inn,
that's the Mississippi in ya'.
Or, when you got a whole lot of cousins,
but yo' mamma and daddy ain't got no brothers or sisters,
that's the Mississippi in ya'.
When you stand 'cause a woman approaches yo' table,
that's the Mississippi in ya'.
When you refuse to call a woman
after ten p.m. or anything but her name,
that's the Mississippi in ya'.
When lovin' your fellow man as you love yo'self
is your political platform, and feedin' little Leroy is your
social welfare program, that's the Mississippi in ya'.
When you pay your bills despite them vampire interest rates,
not because you scared of colorless collectors,
but because yo' granddaddy's word was as solid as the Earth,
and yo' daddy's word is as true as the seasons, and you don't
want to drive down the value of your family's name by being
as unreliable as a politician's promise the day after election,
that's the Mississippi in ya'.
And when you do unto others as you would have them do
unto you because it pleases God and yo' grandmamma,
that's the Mississippi in ya'.

Manifestation

The thumb is a trope and a street sign of evolution
as shades of skin are tied to geographic movement.
Change is the only dominant strain of our DNA.
Like crabs we exchange shells so our souls can flourish.
Those who understand know that we came to go,
bipedal clay endlessly transforming in the hands of
an Omnipotent Poet from potential to kinetic becoming
the Art that the Master Blacksmith molds us to be.
Manifestation (excrement into fertilizer),
transformation, (worms becoming butterflies)
evolution (hunters become gatherers),
transcendentalization (cave dwellers embrace niggers)
God is a climaxing cement mixer.
When He finishes paving the road,
on whose street will you drive?

Like a self-winding clock,
the planets are rectifying the order,
chaos is losing its grip on the lives
of those with the knowledge of how to deconstruct
and diagram spiritual semantics.
There is a rainbow forming in the revelation
that Truth, like sunshine, has walked with us all our lives.
Everything is in seven; cycles are the intestines of life.
God's hand sweeps out across the Black infinity,
fertilizing the minds of his children, spawning seeds of
veracity, making them ready for revolution.
When the holy horn blasts on the one,
and God's funk is ordering the universe,
on what beat will you be standing?
Tomorrow is Today as Now becomes Forever.
Manifestation (one person sitting causes the rest of us to
                stand),
transformation, (rocks become diamonds)
evolution (hitters and hurters become healers),
transcendentalization (truths finally become as self-evident
                as the noses on our faces),
God is an architect.

When He finishes laying the bricks,
in whose house will you live?

The whisper of Love sends a loud shaking
through the dense cosmos.
God igniting the engine for the events of His return.
To find the bull's eye of Truth we must seek
with the audio-visual media of our souls.
When you are bare, are you naked or nude?
Before the universe can you stand
from under the cover of the flesh?
Death no longer wields power like an absentee landlord.
New rivers rushing is God watering the seeds
of his covenant.
Man's frail ideology can't hold back
the locomotive of God's Truth.
Manifestation (one man's death allows the rest of us to
                live),
transformation (white lions sleep with black lambs),
evolution (*Genesis* is our Family Record),
transcendentalization (man walks on water
                      and rides the wheel in the sky),
God is a master contractor.
When He finishes building,
in whose mansion will you live?

Premature (Anti-Climax)

If you love me,
why do you pull the salt water from my eyes?
"But are your tears real?
[i] make you cry tears of joy."
Then why does it hurt?
"The heart was not created for this joy…"
[i] love you so much.
May [i] taste you, or shall you go first?
"It doesn't matter. We both shall drink our fill."
Do you cry for me? "Yes love."
Then lets cry the night into a river of memories,
washing the laundry of our pain…
Kiss me; feel the pillow of my emotions
with the palms of your soul.
Touch me with your love. "Not there, shit!"
Is it happening? Hold on.
[i] think that [i] can see the Dawn.
The pressure's mounting like
hot water in a frozen balloon.
Stop! [i] can't take it.
[i] love you like an existential Christian.
Lovxetsul???
Three words blurred in the babble of our flesh,
amalgamated in our premature souls.
[i]'m finished. Thank you.
Good-bye.

Tangible Documentation

[i] want to be able to point to something
and see what my life is in Technicolor.
[i] want something onto which to hang my hat
like Mr. Rogers' sweater rack or Linus' blue blanket.
[i] wanna be scrolled like the *Book of the Dead*.
My life should be a dessert into which hungry recorders
can sink their teeth and taste the sugary peach fruit
of my labors.
[i] want something on which [i] can call
and hear the blaring, bugling response of my history,
played in the silvery key of significance.
[i] want something that my flaring nostrils can whiff
and smell the earthy rich soil deeds of my actions.
Interpretation eats like cotton candy, and analysis only
presents the ingredients of my life without the flavor.
[i] need a meat and potatoes body of work,
the actions of my life as a bulky thing to be held.
You can keep the causes, reasons, and justifications,
which are merely afterthought seasonings.
[i] need the textual tangible thing that one can
open, unfold, unlock, unzip, unsnap, playback, rewind,
fast forward, mark for later, put on reserve, checkout,
even put on lay-away, finance, or charge.
[i] need something that is the weight of my ways
that defines and marks out its space like stone tablets.
[i] need my life as matter.
It has to be a matter if it's going to matter.
For, [i] have been an empty space between periods
a dash between dates with no story to tell
if there are no files that bookmark my being.

The Hug

Because of your hug, last night [i] wore my shirt to sleep.
Your soul's perfume embedded itself in my
garment's fabric, deep into the textile of my mind.
Like a fanged symbiont, your pheromone
burrowed into the depths of my soul.
One whiff of you, and [i] am back ten calendars ago,
standing on your porch, swimming in the windows
of your soul, thinking to myself that [i] could keep your
commandments if [i] could combine forever to you.
With one hug, Time becomes a willing statue
at a point where my rusted antiquity and my
shinning contemporary converge as one perfect medal
under the molding pressure of the alchemy of your embrace
with all boxes, boundaries, and beliefs
of who [i] am being reedited and rewritten.

You were so callow, and [i] was so carnal.
Like the spiritual schizophrenic that [i] am,
[i] didn't know the difference between sacred and secular.
[i] just kept gazing into your eyes, telling you
how badly [i] wanted to consummate my notions.
Maybe if we were older, we would have realized
that my erection was merely a manifestation
of my need to make you the Madonna of my posterity.
But, [i] was a romantic dyslexic.

It's amazing what hugs can do, how libidinous tension
can be released like raging rivers or articulated like a well-
written thesis simply by an embrace or a squeeze,
two bodies pushing together as close as smoke to fire,
slightly moving and circling just enough to say
"[i]'m still available," or "[i]'m interested,"
or "[i] miss you," or "We could have been good."
So, you both stand there lost in the suffocating space
of the hug, choking on the smoke of memory,
tempting each other to "squeeze a little tighter."

Standing here a decade removed,

looking, again, into your brown pools of sight,
my soul cries a waterfall to soothe my regret,
needing, still, to be baptized in the Gulf of you.
Though we never were a "we," you always belonged to me,
and the distance of Time's walls and winds
has failed to erode the hieroglyphics of the heart
etched deep into the stones of who we are.
With our hug, two healing hearts expand and converge
in a slow throbbing motion, lightly touching the years of
caged emotion beginning to fume, smolder, and blaze with
the slightest touch of our bodies slowly rubbing
against each other like summer fire wood.

[i] look into the lair of your thesis
through your optic windows.
It is then that [i] realize that lost years,
like rotted fire wood,
cannot rekindle or maintain a flame.
They cannot be retrieved like lost files
nor set right by tape, nails, and superglue.
We are two lovers who missed an opportunity to love,
two ships who've gone too far to turn around.
This hug is merely a Spring flower that dies by June.

Ghetto Psychedelica

My Sears Tower Apex is lower than
everybody else's bottom floor basement.
That's because my elevator's erection begins in Hell
and prematurely peaks in Purgatory's penal colony.
Everything [i] got is second hand.
All of my clothes are bastard residents of
Thriftco, Goodwill, and Salvation Army-land.
[i] continuously experience swift moments
of faded, pale yellow Truth;
take another puff and realize that
it's just the high altitude of the roof
and find that my utopia
is merely a dulled, clouded illusion
that fades as quickly as the Easter snap.
Inner peace is a Jezebel.
She cums and leaves me; simultaneously
she taunts, teases, and briefly pleases me.
[i]'m her confused concubine 'cause
[i] give it up so easily like flowers
that bloom at the first touch of the Sun
forgetting that winter's last breath will surely come.
Steady looking for Plato's city,
settling for Ghetto Psychedelica.

Come on

Excuse me, but [i] was wondering if [i] could talk to you. No? Why not? All [i] want is a heartbeat. Who knows, maybe it could trumpet a song to last a lifetime—okay, maybe a night. But it's more than you've ever had. [i]'m sorry. Nice dress. Can [i] wear it? See, [i] have these feelings floating butterfly-like inside me. [i] just wanna know do you have the same feelings that [i] do running like a river inside you. So if [i] feel what you feel, [i] can make you feel the top of your mountain. Oh, that's lame? But [i]'d be wrong to say that every time [i] see you [i] form a tent in my pants? What do [i] want? [i] want to fertilize your soul with mine. You do know how to make love without sex, don't you? It's easy. Just let your emotions walk on the outside of your body. Feel their little feet dancing up and own your spine. Then you can kiss whatever you want. Yes, even that. How does it taste? Was it as satisfying as soul food? Yeah, [i] thought so. Do [i] love you? What do you mean by love, exactly? Define it? My definition?...Well, it's wanting to be with you even when there is nothing to do. But, it is the doing that becomes confusing...[i] don't need to know much. [i] know enough, enough to know that [i] don't love you. Sorry...

Just a Thought of You...

...every time [i] see you, you seem a hologram
of whom you are, a flat two-dimensional
projection on a wall.
You always seem to be somewhere you ain't.
Only your dancing and darting eyes tell that there's
so much more going on wherever your mind is.
Your body creeps along turtle-like
as your eyes remain fixed inward,
shining a light down your dark tunnel.

[i] would like to run up behind you and go "boo,"
just to see what you would do.
But a sliced glanced or a sunset fading stare
is all the time you would endure.
And just as quickly as a mouse returning to its hole,
you'd disappear deep within your hidden self's space.

But beneath your blouse
there is a pounding that
lets me know that life
has a pulse somewhere.
And if [i] could, [i]'d get you
to take me to the chambers of your pyramid
'cause [i] wanna know
what book you're reading
when [i]'m reading you.

The Workout (Metaphysical Metamorphosis)

Cold icicle burns streak along the insides of my
reddening, knotted muscles.
Series of little round sweat beads plop heavily into my eyes
burning the vision of smoke-filled change.

Another repetition,
sets of tens domino through my mind
as [i] jerk and wobble like a twig tree in the wind
to the inhales and exhales of my trembling lungs.
The clang of iron weights against each other
echoes through my hollow inner,
and the beat of left over right pounding the pavement;
it's a symphony of fitness.
It's mind over matter, and matter is all that's on my mind.

More repetitions,
weights being pulled up and down in a rebellion
against gravity's fascist law, the body struggles
like a rowboat moving upstream in a typhoon.
Minutes reluctantly give way to hours
as you are reintroduced to last night's snack,
and at a slight gaze,
the room tilts and warps to the right.
My matter and its nemesis converge
at a spot where a new me is being harvested.

The body is coming through the womb.
The African deity of fitness stands over you,
his body all the reminder that you need,
motivating you to a faint portrait of the future
as the bulge battle continues.
The straw hut that is your mind plays an old song,
a melody of "can't go on," but the newly hardened
concrete will of your soul pushes your outside
to lift one more dumbbell of anxiety,
to run one more step in the direction of liberty.
You feel your old crumbling body
slipping like bad times into darkness,

your new body being reborn like a slow butterfly.
This clay reworking of the potter's hands pains.
Your insides turn and converge, twist and harden;
You can see yourself in the newly cleaned mirror.

As everything goes Black,
your mind slides into the bosom of the darkness
as your body shifts to autopilot
and completes your landing into a field of change.
Your rubbery limbs go limp with a
cardiac arrest of the body,
and death has a key to your door, is turning the knob,
until the center of your ear hears "and relax."

There is no serenity.
You are awakened by cemented muscles and glued joints.
The only way to escape the pain
is to swim toward its mouth.
You are addicted: pain if you do, pain if you don't.

All of this for a flat stomach and a jerked ego?
Ain't that a trip? Is it vanity or insanity?
The seeds of the soul and mind cannot grow
if rooted in a decaying warehouse.

"What a piece of work is man! How noble in reason! how infinite in faculties! in form and moving, how express and admirable! in action how like an angel! in apprehension, how like a god! the beauty of the world! the paragon of animals! And yet, to me, what is this quintessence of dust? Man delights not me; no, nor woman neither…"

William Shakespeare—
from *Hamlet* (II, ii, 115-117)

Oh, How like God We Are?

"Click!" And lightening is snatched from its
place in the sky, drained from the universe,
captured, conducted, controlled, and channeled
like a domesticated animal.
With a flick of the "on" switch,
there is a beacon of burning bright,
man's inner world illuminated,
controlling what he did not create.

"Twist!" And water (a wild roaming herd)
is sucked from its place, rushed like cattle to a point,
stopped and purified (Muddy Waters to Pat Boone)
At a turn, it splashes and drops, a washing machine
for man's inside dirt.

…oh how like God we are…

Sucked, pulled from the decayed remnants of history,
churning like butter waste into energy,
making hot spring from cold winter,
piping from the bowels of Earth,
the gas of rejuvenation,
the oil of lifecycle,
the warmth of life's ground blood.

We hold the organs of Nature
centered in our palm for our pleasure.

This is our ability to mold Nature like pottery
to re-create creation for our own dreams,
making a god out of man.
All the while the pink insides of
babies' bellies bleed with hunger.
Education is withheld breast milk.
The Land Gods have decided so.
Raising spaceships is more precious
than raising babies, and
the educational system is traded
like an old jalopy for the new
sleeker model of juvenile youth court
and the highway of schoolhouse to jailhouse
as we swap Principals for Judges.
We invest our evolution
in jail cells rather than classrooms,
while creationists condemn the criminally educated
and create a capital gains tax.

…oh, how like God we are…?

Root Beer Floats and Chicken Wings

Like musical chefs ordering flavorful notes,
[i] make root beer floats, buffalo shrimp, and
chicken wings with my wife on Friday nights.
Fat calories galore, running wild like bad-ass children!!!
But, that concern is a fading breeze.
We're just happy to be baptized in the midst of each other,
like two kids for whom recess never ends.
She's got hot wing sauce and float residue on her
chin and cheek, a perfectly painted abstraction of
adolescence swirling within maturity—
a golden nymph child with antiquity's platinum soul—
and her eyes a fairytale of happily ever after.
[i] kiss her on her cheek to taste the sauce and her skin.
We sit around in nothing at all, chicken almost gone, and
laugh at ourselves, the sound flowing like a new year's eve
serenade undressing new adventures.

Her overbite is the most precious thing
that [i]'ve ever seen—the manner in which snowflakes
and fingerprints tell us that perfection is finding the proper
peg for your misshaped hole.
Yet, before she can say she wants a child,
[i] feed her another chicken wing.
And with her chiffon soft hands, she places
another shrimp on my eager soaked lips.
Fruit just doesn't seem fit for Friday night,
which is a festival celebrating seven-day survival.
This is that pebble of a moment in time;
the dragon of bills have been slain—at least for the month.
The night is absent of street corner fireworks.
It's just us on the consoling couch keeping company
with well-read books and an old "black and white."
She's watching a tape; [i]'m watching her.
Tomorrow is the Sabbath.
She'll cling to her covers,
and [i]'ll sunrise to write poetry.
But, tonight it's just a two-heart communion
of us, root beer floats, and chicken wings.

All Is never Lost

All in this four-seasoned play is never lost,
because our pockets are too small to hold it all.
When the pain in your red organ
is fatter than the ideas in your thinking room,
you must look to the Light that shines
even when your eyes are closed.
And remember,
All in never gained, so
all is never lost.

See ya'.

If

If is only a blank canvas. But, without if,
actuality would be an old car on blocks.
If is the voodoo or juju of the scientific equation—
the pink and purple magical dust that the numbers need
to plot planetary motion or the waters needed to sail from
the bank of questions to the shore of answers.
For if is the sperm of reality,
fertilizing the eggs of the ideal,
if and only if "if" is freed from the cages of finite dreams.
Never bet the odds against if;
for if you do, you'll be confined to the pockets of the past.
If is organic to man's movement
up metaphysical mountains.
When if plays its guitar, evolution is
a hit song played on everybody's radio.
If is the water to our grass.
And if we sleep without dreams, we fall.
Can't you hear the jingling ring-tone of if?
Answer if, if you care to be a daredevil for change.
Show the if, if you can be
a drum major for the second coming.
Do you care to dare?
Do you dare to care?
Can you stand bare?
Are you real if you are bare?
'Cause if you leave if, you shall be unaware
of the continuous shifting of the universe
through the Big Bang of if.
To dream with if is to plant the seeds
to meet yourself on the other side.
Only through if can we navigate destiny's ship.
Can't you see if when the sun rises?
Sheer energy, soulful electricity—
dive into the sea of if
and give genesis to your mind.
It's time for a new racekind.
If can lead you through the dark halls of doubt.
For if is the master key

to unlock the final chapter of Humpty Dumpty
being pieced together.
Let if take you and impregnate your mind.
Let if drive you through the wormholes of time.
Glorio-fabuo-tabulous if.
All about the realm it will sift,
opening doors, finding the rifts.
If is looking for hearts as free as the wind
and minds lathered of rain liberated from clouds
to plot the universe's constellation to infinity.
It's Freud's equation to a James Brown groove.
If you believe, you will be no Peter on the water.
For dreams no longer deferred will float instead of fall.
Dig the if; explore y'all!
So if "if" is what you have,
the if is there for the growing,
the willing are the showing.
For if makes the lost the knowing.
There is no fear in the if because the reward
for flying is greater than the pain of falling.
As if is indigenous to creation,
if is in itself a constant waterfall of revelation.

If controls the brightness of the picture that you will paint. By unlocking the colorful combinations of your mind, you shall have a funkalicious good time! Yet, if must be found from the inside out. Pour if into your cup and drink all of it. Life without if is merely a calendar with no numbers. Whatever you do, don't let the world lose its if…

Psychedelic

When knowledge is a drug
that explodes like a wet dream,
satisfying more than
any capitalist could ever dream.
When embarrassment is a condition
that is as extinct as dinosaurs and small pox
and fear is a brief memory that faded
like Mississippi's forgotten winter's snow, faded
like Reconstruction after the withdrawal of federal troops.

When a blunt is a poem
and the only white horse you ride
comes with pages and end notes.
When being beamed up by Scotty
is allowing picture words
to help you find your own sublime,
and your epiphany is a river flowing spiritual orgasm,
this is when you're living psychedelic.

When you ain't got no guilt
'cause love is the only money you desire.
And instead of worrying about Wells Fargo,
you're only concerned with how much
money you put in the bank of heaven.
It's then and only then, that you truly know
the secrets of the sign of seven.

When tomorrow is just another day
to find somebody to love,
when you can sleep at night
because you've done everybody right,
you're living psychedelic.

When getting high is getting and giving love,
this is so funky that you got to
roll it up, lick it, and pass it around.
It's the first domino to human salvation,
comes when Love mates with Revelation

and you see the same drab daily things like new creations
because Truth is a new can of paint,
and no matter how high you get
you still understand that you must come before you go.
And giving it away is what you've been living for,
being wrapped in a rainbow
for now and forever more.

Bathing in the silk tears of God,
baptized, your light will be a body spray
that will forever glow
'cause your smile begins
deep in a space where only grace can go.
This is when you realize that your soul is electric;
this is when you're living psychedelic.

Seasons

The crisp intimate coat of winter sensations
of tickling chills prickling the skin like thousands
of tiny frozen feathers, smooth and razor sharp.
The Byronic darkness, days hazed in cotton gray
shortened and made more precious than diamonds.
Cozy-warm nights of hugs bring the rediscovery of corners
and spaces in the house that you had forgotten in summer.
Artificially heated nights, cut with the radiated chill
of bedroom windows brushed from a snowy soft breeze.
The sound of a winter night, wind whistling like a choir
with time kept by a crackling fire, music to move, love, and
slumber by, as the third and fourth cups of unfinished
chocolates perfumes the air
with mystic fantasy and serenity.

Wet, cold rain blows, pushing like Prometheus
the lightly heated breeze of the West.
More rain, and browns begin to undress
into yellows and greens.
The Earth and her creatures re-flower.
Morning dew is the residue of the early morning sex
between Father God and Mother Earth
as He penetrates her soil.
It's the annual wedding, renewing of vows between old
lovers which covers the countryside with pastel life.
The Sun of God's Manhood lightly touches Mother Earth's
erogenous zones, forcing a smile from each living thing.
It's the resurrection, when Nature
pulls back her dress and bears her beauty to man.

Man in perpetual pilgrimage. Highways line with lost and
lingering Canterburians. Motels packed with vacationers.
The body stripped down, erect,
and pushing toward the Sun.
As the heat soothes the muscles of the weary traveler,
sunglasses shade the eyes from the power of God too strong
for man's cloudy winter vision.
Child laughter fills the air like the

fragrance of fresh flowers;
we play in grass diamonds,
chasing pop flies and stealing bags.
Soda pop and a/c are worth more than gold.
Short nights of heated passion are cooled by
central air and soft kisses.
We awake to days that last forever
with eight p.m. sneaking up on us like old college friends.
Summer is the party girl in tight shorts and halter tops,
with full lips and a sensual smile that extends,
"Catch me while you can before [i] go home in August."
So you spend June and July chasing her, catching her for
temporary twinkling of sizzling bliss that forever remain
special memories that warm your inners in winter.

A night train of cool gentle evening breeze against
a hot noon blister taps us on the shoulder,
warning us of winter.
The air smells like football,
new school clothes, and summer good-byes.
"Will you write me?" "Everyday."
"And call on Sunday?" "Surely."
Greyhound and Delta take us home and off to college.
New acquaintances replace old friendships.
Greens fade into brown overcoats.
We waltz into winter.

Seasons (On the Other Side of Town)

An icy biting day puts distance in our eyes,
stabbing us repeatedly like thousands
of large sharpened daggers, slicing through our bodies
intensifying our vexation.
Poe's darkness shadows short frozen days
as night air exposes the cracks in the roof, walls, and floors.
(Landlords are as elusive as night rainbows.)
Howling winter night air
carrying pneumonia in its knapsack crashes against
the shutters, trying to get at you.
Eight children huddle around a third-hand electric heater
with a frazzled chord that fades like a cheap shirt.
They are wide awake and angry with icicles in their bellies,
melting to a brown liquid that seeps into the yard.

Stinky, sticky wetness on top of hounding humidity
reminding you that you have no windows in your car.
And now the grass needs a haircut,
but you're a barber without proper tools,
as every little despicable, nasty, creepy, crawly thing
invades your house like Roman soldiers looking to plunder.
You renew your acquaintance with the smells
of the alley below your cracked kitchen window.
Snow gone, it's the resurrection of the
abandoned cars, un-emptied trash cans,
and boarded up, pissed in houses.
The city pulls back her dress and reveals
that she needs a bath.

It's too hot to move, and you're too broke to do anything.
Grocery stores packed with people
who have no domestic cooling units.
Naked swollen bodies reveal
how some kept warm in the winter.
Others lay covered in sweat and brownish grime.
Head pounds from noisy juveniles
paroled for the summer.
Nights spent on stoops and porches,

swatting flies and mosquitoes
that are big enough to swat back.
We finally sleep in the cool of the dawn.
Summer is a hot little Lolita heifer
causing her lover strokes and heart attacks.
We can't wait 'til the bitch goes home for school.
Memories? All summer days are the same…hot…

Here comes winter as Mr. Do Nothing Autumn
wastes our time with brown nothingness,
acting as a bellhop to winter.
But it's a nice nothing.
Not hot enough to be hot.
Not cold enough to be cold.
Not festive enough to be fun,
but not long enough to matter.
Autumn is oatmeal at its best.
Discount clothes and lay-away,
hopefully we'll get the coats by Christmas.
Mo' new mockingbirds to learn.
We fall into our trap of routine.
Damn, it's winter again!?!

Natural

[i] like sleeping with you when it's raining.
[i] wanna rain inside you as God saturates Mother Nature,
raining down His liquid essence
into her fertile, green grasses.
(Morning dew is so enchanting.)
Like us, they have so many positions as Mother Earth
revolves for God, letting Him wet her all over.
[i] wanna place wet kisses over your landscape,
like God blowing damp winds over the horizon.
Everyday with you is spring, nipples like budding flowers
letting me know that love is in season.
[i] wanna caress your hills and mountains,
play in your valley,
and swim nude in your rivers and streams.
Like bees to flowers, [i] wanna drink your nectar;
[i] wanna pollinate your soul. Like a seasoned farmer
[i] wanna work your Earth with my bare hands.
Like a fiery summer hurricane,
[i] wanna be the change in the weather,
melting your ice caps,
causing your rivers to rush wildly toward me.
Mother Nature come to me and let me be your God.
Can [i] fertilize you, swim up your stream and spawn?
Some days [i] like just laying in your canyon
with my head resting between your alpine region.
Gravity makes us one, pulling me to your core, and [i] can't
keep my kisses away from your equator, tracing your lines.
Every time [i] explore you, [i] find something new.
[i] worship your Earth and all of its regions.
Just call me Estevanico as everyday is another day
to find new treasures across your terrain.
[i] wanna do it with the Sun shining,
so [i] can see all of your flowers.
[i] wanna trace your longitude and your latitude.
With my elongated ruler, [i] wanna plot every each of you,
rediscovering and claiming your body
in the name of spring and reincarnation.
[i] don't need a map 'cause [i] know my way around you,

and without a compass [i] can still find my way
in and out of your deepest caves.
They are all lush and wet with rivers flowing through them.
Are your flowers blooming? Are you ready to blossom?
Is your ice cap melting and your rivers rushing?
Is your soil ready to be cultivated?
My nature, your nature,
natural is the desire for fertilization,
just as leaves slowly turn from brown to green
as butterflies emerge from cocoons
as April showers bring May flowers
as cool winter winds become warm caressing kisses
as animals shed their skin and furs as we shed our clothes
to become as bare as truthful as organic as possible
as the colorful dance of the peacock
as the marvelous sway of your skirt
as the sweet call of the nightingale along a midnight breeze
as the throbbing rise of your hills
underneath a flowing silk blouse
as the scent of the lion on a marked tree
as the smell of your pheromone
mixed with your cinnamon sugar waters
as the loud, boisterous call of the wild
as the tom-tom pounding expansion of my manhood
growing with every single moon of you,
my nature, your nature, as water to its own level…

Memory Child

A washer, a ringer,
a piece of soda pop can
on my finger,
these are the things [i] remember—
housed in the trunk of my mind.
A stage plant, a honey bun,
an open hand begging for some,
but some make you dumb, so you don't need none.
Lemon Heads and Jaw Breakers,
orange and yellow wrestle on a canvass of brown,
blown into a twirl by a windy flatland afternoon.
Smell that rain; a storm's coming soon.
The scent of wet pine needles suffocated by
the odor of heated asphalt and .38 residue.
Haven't smelled the rain since [i]'ve moved to the city.
Removed from Nature my soul is an abandoned house.

A peach, a plum, a piece of bubble gum,
engine, engine number nine going down Chicago line,
rolling getting itchy in the grass,
playing in my school clothes,
mama gon' kill my ass.
Damn, my pants [i] tare because of a dare
now [i] must stand before mama bare.
It's with psalm [i] sing this song
and bid to Eshu and his signifying monkey
to do justice to me;
for that is the tree that shaded and cooled me
'til [i] turned all of twenty-three.
But then expansion came to town,
and capitalism cut my tree down.

Café-Chicken Grease Ass Nigga
(An Ode to my Shadow)

Pork chops and ham samaches, the greasier the better.
That's why you can't use my comb.
[i]'m a still-life of every stereotype [i]'ve ever known.
From all my women, [i]'m just seeking subjugation.
Somebody help me; [i] can't crucify and raise myself;
[i] guess [i]'m just another café-chicken grease ass nigga.

Every suit is as loud as Jimi's guitar.
Every pillow [i]'ve got is stained.
The collars on my shirts can never stay clean.
[i] like my music intrusive when [i]'m riding around,
but [i] turn it down when on the white side of town.
Somebody help me; this quicksand's pulling me down;
[i] guess [i]'m just another highlight on the late night news.
Euro-centrically speaking, [i] love being alone.
[i]'ve cut off bridges to almost everyone [i]'ve ever known.
Can't tell me the square root of nothing. [i]'ve got answers
for answers piled in my pocket like a full diaper.
When my Wile E. Coyote plans fail,
[i]'ve got no problem blaming the Master Architect
even when [i] refuse to follow His blueprint,
and my plans are littered with atrocious Acme products.
Somebody help me; [i]'ve dug a hole with no ladder.
[i] guess [i]'m just another number in DHS's case study.

When [i] look in the mirror, guess what [i] see,
a chicken-grease café nigga with a degree.
Somebody help me; going blind
from the fumes of my perm.
Salvation is stripped away every time [i] relax.
Somebody help me; [i]'m not coming up after three days.
[i] guess [i]'m just another bullet in the foot of my people.

Schizophrenic Tendencies

Always afraid (…) of being (…) found out (…)
like the students who found the teacher's test
or like the Wizard behind the transparent curtain
where Oz has been bulldozed for a parking lot.
Love is a conditional thing based on sanity.
Faint voices, not yet fully articulated…
echo softly in the cracked recesses of my mind.
Looking into the glassy eyes of those who have
already taken their leaves of absences,
searching the lines and blank nothingness of their faces,
hoping for vague clues of my own play's ending.

[i] doubt; therefore, [i] maybe (?)

Memories, like unwanted guests, come
when [i] don't want them to
and eat all of the food of my mind.
[i] apologize for shit that [i] haven't yet done.
Remember me as [i] was or wanted to be,
not as the Frankenstein monster that [i] shall become.

[i] love you. (Something in my brain speaks this.)
             ([i]'ve never known to whom.)
[i] love you. ([i] apologize for my ambiguity)
             ([i]'m still seeing an elephant in my pajamas.)

Mental illness is a beach to the pebble which is AIDS.
Once you've taken a leave of absence,
even if as fleeting as a summer rain,
you are forever the clown in the three-ringed
circus of everyone else's mind.
If your mind is a condemned building,
then you are homeless.
It's basic algebra with no solution for x.

This is not the beautiful picture that hangs
in your grandmother's living room.
Searchin' for Psychedelica can be so gray,

or is that the effect of all of the
brainstormin' from midnight 'til dawn?

Is the cure worse than the illness?
Is the medicine merely a different trip,
another opportunity to turn on, tune in, and cop out?

Last night, night before,
twenty-four robbers knocking at my door.
Whatever you do…Don't let them in!!!

Delayed schizophrenia is sitting on death row
waiting on a death date with no appeals left.
You can hear the phone ringing, but it's not for you.

The mind is a funny thing.

Who wants to be poignant,
especially when the mountain climbers
don't do nothing after the climb but sit there?
[i] thought you didn't get saved to sit down.

Sex is a metaphoric act of the Everyman.
It is the allegory to end all similes.
We all want to come and go at the same time.

Raison Brand and my wife be my only comforts.
Writing tells the (T)ruth; that's no comfort.

Should [i] sit still and wait for the blinding, bright light of
schizophrenia to swarm me like termites?
Or, should [i] go wildly into the light
as the Tasmanian devil that [i] am?

Reality doesn't bother me…

[i] love my wife; however,
[i] don't believe that anyone's heart could beat for me…

Poetry Affliction

The words in my head make my brain harder
than a late night, lonely erection,
and [i] feel like [i]'m gonna explode
if [i] can't jack off some of my literary expressions.
[i] can't get by without my daily orgasm.
And some days [i]'m so horny that [i] need a literary orgy,
keeping my brain climaxing several times over.
Yet, [i] still have books with no covers.

See, you really don't know how a poet thinks
especially when [i] have a mind filled with words
but [i] can't afford the ink.
And the local newspapers won't cover you
'cause you ain't in the *New York Times Book Review*.
See, ain't no need to lie.
For his work, every poet wants to be acknowledge,
but [i] got a disease called can't get published.
Being a poet is like being on crack
'cause no matter how the word mistreats you,
you keep coming back.
In the middle of the night
words whisper promises in your ear,
and to a pen, pad, or computer you must sleep near.
But it's worse than crack 'cause
there ain't no twelve-step program.
[i]'m just a junky looking of a hit
to last me to the next manuscript or open mic set.

[i] got words, phrases, and ideas
mutating into metaphors with claws and fangs.
[i]'m a continuously relapsing case
'cause [i] was born with poetry on the brain.
So many poems, feels like [i] got diarrhea of the mind.
With no relief in sight,
my brain stays horny with little rest a night.
As rejection slips come in the mail,
[i]'m a whore that no one wants to pimp.
So since [i] can't seem to trap any tricks,

[i] decide to prostitute myself.
But [i]'m swimming in quicksand
'cause although [i] need new tires on the car
[i] risk the ride 'cause [i] need some book covers.
And [i] must decide between
fixing the toilet or the printer.
(We'll be pouring water down the drain for a while.)
And [i] know we need toilet tissue, but
ain't no sense fixing the printer
and not getting any printer paper.
So like a biscuit eating dog,
[i] look at my wife who
hasn't been treated like a wife in a while,
and my step-kids who need new soles for school.
All the while poetry
is hounding me like a three a.m. booty call.
And like the other woman on a late night fall,
[i] roll over and answer the call.

When Was the Last Time that You Were Properly Kissed?

When was the last time that you were properly kissed,
when a man with the skill of a surgeon
and the preciseness of a mathematician placed
his peach moist lips against yours
and in that moment of cotton softness you felt
his philanthropic soul brush like feathers against yours,
and in that moment you were caressed in a cloud of kisses?

Did you know that a kiss, if properly done, can
erase fears, answer doubts, and call you home to rest?
Yes, a kiss can be salvation—
sweet, strawberry sensations of salvation.

So, when was the last time that you were properly kissed?

Are you tired of brothers bashing their stone lips against
yours, shoving his uncoordinated tongue down your throat,
grabbing your back person like he's laying bricks
and then calling that foreplay?

Do you wanna be kissed so well that even on a crowded
street you two become the only flowers in the field.
Where would you like the tip of our thoughts to meet?
When was the last time you were properly kissed?

When was the last time that you felt a tongue caress you,
slide down and tickle every landmark of your earth?
When was the last time that your man
rediscovered all of who you are with
his silk fingertips and snake-like tongue,
letting his hands and kisses fall upon you
like leaves and rain in an autumn breeze?

May [i] massage you with my tongue?
[i] wanna lay you down and see how many licks
it takes to get to your center.

When we kiss, [i] want you to close your eyes and
see the shimmering silhouette of a swirling setting sun,
baptizing you in a shower of
tequila tangerines and ravishing red wines.
When we kiss, [i] want you to feel as if
you are swimming nude in the Nile River.
When we kiss, [i] want to have you shaking
like wet flowers in a spring breeze.
When we kiss, [i] want to make love to your mouth.
When we kiss, [i] want my tongue to reach all the way
 down and touch the plush plum pillow of your center.

When was the last time that you were properly kissed?

When [i] place my firm desire against your quivering
anticipation, allowing our tongues to braid us like locks,
feeling the vibration of your heart pounding with every
flick, [i] want our tongues to come together and move
like Debbie Allen to a Miles Davis solo
on a Saturday night.
When we kiss, [i] want to flood both sets of your puckers
from the Niagara Falls of our kisses.
So tell me,
when was the last time that you were properly kissed?

Cool Ranch Doritos/Peanut Butter and Jelly

Cool Ranch Doritos make me re-member my cousin John,
a mountain of memories built with friends, food, and fun.
Two Musketeers making our day
with a Prince CD and a bag of Doritos.
Now we seek separate swashbuckling adventures;
guess that's how life goes. Ain't it a trip how lives diverge
like hidden paths in an unkempt field.
Time becomes China's wall,
our lives segregated by the tracks of change.
Yet, at the end of another day of pulling the mule,
when the Sun of summer is 'bout done,
[i] just eat another Dorito and re-member cousin John.

[i] like peanut butter and jelly
when my plowing day is through.
[i] like peanut butter and jelly like a real man 'spose to.
Eating my favorite sandwich, mouth too full for words
that's when [i] met my first love,
her name was Audrey Curb.
Pigtails and big smiles, love stands before you
and stretches for miles and miles,
like that dirt road that became gravel then paved.
Off to college is where [i] made my way,
building new memories on the construction site of my life,
and Audrey became a river that [i] never saw twice.
But to the gumbo of who [i] am, she's an important spice.
Cool Ranch Doritos—peanut butter and jelly,
such budding times, kid food for our juvenile bellies.
Adolescent plans like sandcastles
fade into the sea of memory,
but the nutrition of youth feeds you forever.

God
1 Jesus Way
The Throne Area, Heaven 00001

Re: Turmoil of the Soul

Dear God:

As you can tell from the irregular beats of my heart, confusion is the song that is playing on my radio, and [i] can't find the starting point of this circle. It seems that [i]'m a scientist with no hypothesis, a mouse in a malicious maze. Up and Down, Left and Right, Right and Wrong change constantly with the seasons of man. [i] twirl like a spin top in the hands of a wayward child. [i] know that you are saying that [i] only know you in times of trouble like an unveiled politician draped in a neon dashiki, double-clutching the *Bible* and the *Koran* like they are credit cards to grace, but that's only because to merely call your name is like washing dirty clothes in Clorox. A Picasso painting pales in comparison to your perfection for you have created raindrops and snowflakes with their own fingerprints. Thus, [i] take you for granted because [i] can count on you to remove the trash from my life any day that [i] set it on the curb. Yet, sleep slips through my mind as sand through my fingers for my mind is a jackrabbit that sleep's hunter fails to target. The video game in my mind never shuts down. Jesus is the raft that [i] need in this ocean of sin that muddies the waters of my den. Is it that [i] have had you on lay-away too long? Are my sins, like delinquent payments, finally catching up with my credit? No matter how fast [i] run, the tortoise is always there, and my enemies use his gaining crawl against me. Father, if [i] cannot be covered in cotton-cloth peace, make my mind a blank chalkboard. Delete the CPU of my soul; no, make me able to return the gaze of my mirrored image.

Your child,
C. Liegh

Something Strange

Cosmic explosions of electricity bubbling under the
reservations of my mind, tingling sensations dancing down
my spine while the raspberry moon and purple stars
funk a jam of nuclear compounds merging into gyrating
chocolate covered emotions, causing my heart to pound to
your bass line as our eyes dart and dance the jitterbug every
time we meet while the wind echoes a pumping passion of
Black…(Don't you wanna come around my tree?)
We could do something the other animals want to see.
My misgivings are melted by your smile's solution.
When [i]'m in your space,
[i] wanna put round in square;
[i] wanna put on clothes that no one else would wear.
[i] wanna make strange the new Black.

Tiny, prickling time bombs pregnant with possibilities set
off in my mind, a rainbow of orgasms against the satin
Black canvass of Time, cherries, blueberries, and
pineapples weave a tapestry of light that shines my reaction
to the synthesis of your sweet stuff winding down the
seventh corner of my mind
unlocking visions to a very funky time.
As elephants tip toe through the flowers unseen by the
blind man in the ivory tower, neon scenes constantly
converge and change, and in the geometry of my mind
with you [i] wanna do something strange.

…and Love walked to the edge of its own mind and created, pulling from the wet womb of its own self the chord to infinity.

Thinking

If [i] had your mind, and you had mine,
who would be better off?
Isn't it a race-car, roll-a-coaster thought
that all people aren't carbon copies.
But [i] know that you would be
better off with the library of my mind.
Then you would paint as [i].
But [i] would also record your favorite shows.
We would still be driving in different lanes.
But my river for you will still flow
toward your equator,
which means that your bass would still
swim up my stream and spawn.
Wouldn't that be nice?

Psychedelica

And the world goes…
the spinning is a symbol of having somewhere to be.
Psychedelica, natural Funk as organic as maize for your soul.
Dreams on the other side trying to seduce
the limp, seedless reality of this side.
If [i] look deeply into the broken mirror of life,
[i] can see the "me" that [i]'m supposed to be.
Plotting the coordinates of my back-road journey
as the mirror's glass becomes liquid,
color is the only saving grace;
for Black is the canvass of creativity
where rainbows converge in
endless orgies of funktasia.

Doors only close
so that others may be opened.
You just have to find the door knobs.
The eyes in your head
are too impotent to see the light.
Your soul has a compass
that'll guide you through the murky swamps of doubt
to the fresh water of the Dawn.

Psychedelica is a woman…
sister of Dawn, mother of Ebullience.
With a brush, a caress, and a kiss,
you will come.
Psychedelica is a woman,
let her give birth to your Republic.

To Get Wild in the Nile

As she licked moist lips dripping with the
wet dreams of a people longing to be free,
her eyes smiled a "That's the way [i] like it"
under the cover of sky crocheted in orange and Black
cascading off the brown sand pregnant with history
with the moon half way down the backside of the night.
We can do it on a dew ground.
With nature's flute lullaby adrift in the air,
[i] can with my damp dreams lick your tummy.
No need for a hot comb, your ancient beauty is what [i]'m
about, just one night of drinking your flowing emotions
on the grounds where Isis is raised, the divinity trinity
makes a child, the three of us: you, me, and the Nile.

How about some fruit, love?
[i] like to suck sweet, sticky fingers.
[i]'ll offer up my sacrifice to ensure your salvation.
Not just your body, [i] want your soul's mind.
Like it used to be in 6000 BC, before pimping was more
than a striding pace, before you forgot the rib we share,
when we were the protoplast of God's painting.
Let's make love like we know we are the first.

Let's make love so hard that our bodies carve the Truth like
living hieroglyphics on the wall of humanity's *Book of Life*.
Let's procreate, re-create the time before
the Garden was rezoned and redeveloped.
If we do it right,
God's story will be read in the flowering of our seeds
in a language that reclaims our rightful place in glory.
[i]'m your man, your Father-God; you're my Mother Earth,
to the Egyptians behind the mirror waiting for us to finally
see the map that's been burned in our bodies,
let our love pollinate rebirth.
In one perfect orgasm, we send the flood waters
that wash away the lies of the cave dwellers
and fertilize the soil for the Sun's new children.

On the Eve of Suicide

…did you ever want to have warm words of
relief written on the papyrus of your soul,
but no soul had ears for you?
You are an archeologist digging for connection,
but no soul has ears for you.
Is life just some well constructed tragedy
for some old dude with a well-groomed white beard
sitting around his popcorn eating angles
watching us like some wound-up clock
(theatre of the absurd)
with a continuous plot of to be continued?
Or, is it a shaky ground tale where
volleyballs make excellent flat characters,
which, for practical purposes,
is a bit better than the force that pushes Bigger.
Yet in all three plays, we are mere puppets
that have only an earthen trunk waiting for us.
Stories told by no one, for nothing.
[i] guess [i] should be scared,
a scarecrow surrounded by steroid laced swans,
but [i] passed scared when [i] crossed
the state line of lonely
for having no soul with which to convene.
God doesn't count.
His *deus ex machina* doesn't travel like it use to.
[i] need someone whose hands reek with the slop stench
of reality—even Celie's Mister knows transformation,
resurrection if you will…
[i] need someone whose feet trace the same mud
whose toenails grow the same fungus as mine.
Jesus wore the flesh's overcoat, but
it was never strapped to His mortality.
Did He reality understand how isolating the body can be?
Jesus, they tell me you cried.
For whom did your rivers flow?
Your eye water is too sanitized if they were for me.
Do you know what it's like to baptize your own sorrows?

For the Enlightened One

How does it feel to be a wave in the universe's ocean?
From across the room, [i] bathe in you.
[i] gaze and drown in your beautiful brown;
it's an oak nut marble hue (tree of forever)
which covers your jaguar features
like strawberries dipped in fudge chocolate.
[i]'m afflicted badly with you
dying from the silent pneumonia of your grace.

[i] could never be the garrison you need me to be.
For your feet remain planted in the grass of Truth,
your head above the clouds seeking the cradle of divinity.
And [i] am too drunk on my male-factor,
my mind too permed to see through
the fumes of masculinity.
You need a Monarch not a drudge.
In my feeble flesh and twig like bones,
[i] could not suitably serve you up to God,
never being able to properly cleanse your feet.

You are the brightest star in our universe,
the fertile soil of the Earth.
You make me want to till lands.
[i] want to touch the lips
of my psyche against yours,
using my erect reason
to trace the outline of your space.

May [i] wash you?

[i] long to draw your bath
with piping hot water and big blue bubbles,
using my bare, soap covered hands to
wash away the dirt of our race's failed plans,
covering your brown in lavender lather,
then scooping two sultry and soft handfuls of water,
pouring it out over you like a waterfall of justice
so that it cascades down, rinsing away the residue

of your daily dirty battles to flush our minds.
Then, [i]'ll wrap your inners in a cotton towel,
placing you on a bed of antiquity,
feeding you fudge and fruits
and reading to you until the Dawn of humanity rises.
(Your soul is so complete that sex is a distraction.)
Your voice soothes me like a skilled masseuse.
[i] can't tell you how many orgasms
your words have forced my mind to have.
You are the river Jordan as your poetry
pierces and cleanses my soul.
[i] climax with every word that
passes across your liquid-soft caramel lips.

But your words are too heavy for my frail, fragile essence.
You are a Matriarch, and [i] am a pauper.
So, [i]'ll continue to watch you
through our window of separation,
climaxing from the ejaculations of your brain.

History Lesson

Truth is…
Evolution is as inevitable to humanity
as gravity is to sagging breasts.
We are all singular-soul organisms,
making our way back to Adam's den.
We are a complex molecule of Beauty and Science
which divides and gives birth to Meaning.
Beauty is the butterfly leaving the cocoon,
and Science is understanding that
death is the womb to the eternal,
returning infinitely better to be Man and Wholeman,
but the sunlight of knowledge
is hidden by the smog of Hate.
We lose our focus to the thick,
sweet, saucy, seductive smell of tyranny,
forgetting that Black and White are merely bookends
for life's spectrum of hues, as rain and sunshine
are both needed to make plants grow;
for all colors are cousins needing each other to breed.
When was the last time that you danced with Roy G. Biv,
his crayons caressing your soul like silk,
making you know that the circle remains unbroken
when everyone paints?
Who built the DNA pyramids of Time
is the question that gets lost in the blustery wind
of corroded college curriculums, creating eroding,
murky, milky minds with too many numbing degrees
polluted in barren soil, as the echoing cries and pleas
of ancient civilizations fall on rusted, deaf ears.

As many times as it rains, God reveals himself to us,
but our pitiful, pathetic, penis and pussy filled minds
can't see God 'cause we'd rather fuck than pray.

We never learn to bridge the gap
between walking and flying
because we've failed to learn that
the color of Truth is Truth.

So we keep smoking sass, settling for that temporary hit,
believing in grades and diplomas instead of
knowledge and wisdom for our salvation,
not knowing that the ultimate A
comes from completing God's curriculum.

Turning from Nature, we turn toward hollow humanities.
Philosophy is a reason to remove God from the sky
and put Love on a payment plan
as logic sweetens our inequities like lemonade,
swinging ethics through a revolving door of convenience:
"It's okay to wear dirty draws
if some else wears dirty draws."
Our education causes us to act rationally foolish,
loving a God whom we do not see,
hating man whom we dare not see,
too blind to see God's image when our unfocused eyes
fall upon human bodies reduced to chattel,
thus constructing white walls
that separate man from humanity,
then blaming the Son of Man for our ass-backward actions.

There are only two rules.
Number one, don't do shit to anybody
that you don't want done to you
'cause the universe is a mathematical equation,
and the shit that you do will come back to you
like a big ass ghetto boomerang.
Rule number two, which is really the alpha rule,
don't put shit before God
'cause on a cold winter's morning,
that Lexus won't start.
Then it'll be too late to catch a ride on Ezekiel's chariot,
and your friends will leave your
black and blue ass in Satan's sallow snow.

We live in a world of color and despise
the salad bowl of our kaleidoscopic lives.
We live in a world of duality,
and continue to flatten it into our fifties mentality.

How have we evolved with such petty proclivity?

[i]'m a Mississippi boy corrupted by cable.
The notion of integrated riches is like a worm
burying a hole into my apple's core of inner peace.
Yet, [i]'m civilized because
[i] can program a VCR?

Egyptians got high. Asians got high.
Greeks got high. Romans got high.
Jews got high. Arabs got high.
Native Americans damn sho' got high.
All these children chasing the same God
but can't see their fellow travelers
for the fog of their fear.

Do you hang with Jesus or roll with Muhammad,
chill with Buddha or search the Taoist clouds?
Are you a conformist like Confucius,
or trying to bottle the déjà vu of the Hindu?
Have you read your H.I.P., Holy Instruction Pamphlet,
from cover to cover?
Or, are you trying to cook with no recipe,
and then complain when you burn the meal?
How are you going to find the gold without a map?
Maybe you'll be like Columbus
and make the shit up as you go,
but [i] doubt if God can be contextualized or colonized.

Next time, will you be in the crowd begging for Barabbas?

> "What happens to a dream deferred?"
> from "Harlem" by Langston Hughes

The Wait

We are all at the dock,
waiting on somebody else's ship to claim.
We are all at home, waiting on Ed McMahon
to give us our neighbor's check.
We are all in a hurry to wait: waiting to get some,
hurry to fall in love and then wait by the phone,
waiting for someone to love us back.

We are in a constant state of under-satisfaction
which leads to the un-satisfaction
> of not getting enough to eat
which leads to the dissatisfaction
> of not liking the meal prepared to eat
which leads to the frustration
> of not knowing how to cook
which leads to the restlessness
> of waiting on someone to cook
which leads to chaos
> from having waited too long.

Waiting to be happy, putting the soul's fulfillment in a
storage box to play with the pleasures of the body.
We major in the "Pop Life"
to euthanize our fall from grace,
the secular dissection of the soul from the body,
the human from humanity, man from God
'causing us to only know the second half of the movie
as we wait on the other half
in a theatre with no reels,
passing time with temporary fixes
and previews that never come.

Since Adam's and Eve's divorce from the Garden,
we've been waiting,
aimlessly roaming and wondering

like the lost Tribe of Israel,
trying to find the four rivers on a flawed map.
Our inner compass is broken.
Like an egotistical husband, we take no directions,
yet we wait by the phone with a blank face
a morbid, horizontal line for a mouth,
two rounded, smoked eyes,
a face devoid of character lines,
sunken like raisons with Time,
waiting on today to blossom into tomorrow.

Growing tired of waiting,
we answer any call:
wrong numbers, crank calls,
people trying to sell us something.
We'll talk to anybody to relieve the pain.

And as we wait, Time becomes an ambiguous wind;
the gangrene of boredom sets in.
We forget that we are waiting,
and become planted in the wrong garden,
suffocated by the weeds of content.

[i] Will not Pimp Poetry

Right and Wrong, for me, are often
as interchangeable as the pieces of a Mr. Potato Head.
Cheating, stealing, and scheming is what you are doing
only if you are found with your hand in the cookie jar.
Yet, even with the checkered stains
on the shirts of my past,
there is one thing that [i] will never do;
As long as the sun chases the moon,
[i] will never pimp poetry.

[i] will not tell a sister
"Say girl, your poetry is really tight,"
when all [i]'m really thinking is
"How can [i] get you home tonight?"
And [i] will not tell her how much [i] was moved by
the power and imagery of her metaphors and similes
when what [i] really want to do is suck her…
[i] will not pimp poetry.
If [i] want to fornicate with you,
[i]'m gonna tell you that
[i] wanna fornicate with you
'cause to poetry like the tides to the moon
this brother must always be true.

Poetry is not a whore for me to whip out when it's
convenient to get digits or the panties.
Poetry is not a uniform that affirms
to some secret group [i] belong.
Poetry is not a credit card.
Poetry is not a German engineered driving machine
used to compensate for my lack of prowess.
Poetry is not a secret handshake.
Poetry will not write your name
in the *Lamb's Book of Life*.

Poetry is simply the Ritilan that keeps the
teeter-tooter see-saw world from
plunging me headlong into the sandbox of insanity,

keeping me from going atop some roof
and firing until everyone is dead
or [i]'m out of bullets,
which is why [i] cannot pimp poetry.

[i] will not have more *Cliff Notes*
in my house than books.
[i] will not spend time in front of the mirror learning how
to properly place my lips to enunciate words while
spending little time churning those terms in the factory of
my mind until [i] have produce a liquid understanding.
[i] will not recite "The Revolution Will not Be Televised"
when [i] spend my time watching the revolution of the
absurd in the three-ring circus of Jerry Springer.
[i] will not pimp poetry.
[i] will not tell you that [i]'m from New York City
when [i] know my barefoot walking ass is from
Clarksdale, Mississippi.
Can your mind take its numb fingers and feel me,
or are you to busy trying to perpetrate a thief of artistry?
Like your grandma's living room,
do you respect poetry, or
are you just trying to get some diggity?

Until [i] See You Smile Again
(For a Departed One)

You were as comfortable in your skin
as a baby in his mother's arms.
Uniquely you, painting the "I" in individuality
and hanging it on a wall that we could all share.
With a smile that lit up the night sky,
sad moments were as brief as Mississippi winters
when you were near.
[i]'ll always rewind in my mind how your
sun sweetened, joyous juice filled words
would fall gently on my ear like rain in a desert.
Your life is a pyramid to be seen by generations.
[i]'ll hold you in my heart like oxygen in my lungs
until [i] see you smile again.

Like a noun and its infinite positions
you held every post designed for a male
like an essential part of speech to the
language of our lives.
Or like a verb you were our action and being
conjugating us to diagram our possibilities.
Our lives are more articulate because of you.
Now, [i] know that your smile is now a star
that gives heaven its gentle radiance.
Like a nova, the shine of your brief life
will streak our skies for a lifetime.
Your deeds are a river that will never dry.
[i]'ll hold you in my heart like water to vegetation
until [i] see you smile again.

You Still Stimulate my Nasty
(Inspired by the Psychedelica of my Wife)

After all the suns and moons we've seen, my desire still
hungers for the southern sweetness of your buttery yams.
Being in the midst of you is like being with three
'cause no one but you stimulates my nasty.

All [i] have to do is think of you
and wild horses begin to stampede in my pants.
[i] like watching you from behind
when you are washing dishes.
The way your gown static clings to you,
making a silhouette of your shimmering glory
as you neck is the equator to the river of my kisses.
Positive and negative,
your female is a magnet for my male.
[i] want to drink you.
[i] want to pour you into a glass, raise you to my lips,
and swallow every drop of your tangy nectar.
[i] love the flowery smell of you
when my tongue turns your river into an ocean,
as you expand and contract around me.
Your musical moans are a beacon
leading me deeper into the cave of your soul.

Girl, can't you see;
just to hear you breathe stimulates my nasty.

[i] still get off on our bedroom noise,
our worn ass mattress and our scratched-up headboard
banging and clanging against the wall,
like a locomotive churning coal into energy.
(They won't be able to rent this chamber for a while.)

After the mountains of our years,
[i] know your spot like the dents of our bed,
and every time [i] hit it, it's like finding it for the first time.
As your stream is flowing, [i] want to bathe in you,
washing myself in your waters.

Please, baptize me in your holy river.

Do you know what [i] want to be?
([i]'m clay for your thoughts.)
Do you know what [i] want to do?
([i]'m a river that bends for you.)
Do you know what [i] want to kiss?
(My mouth is a magnet to you.)
And [i]'ll give you a cup of kisses to cool your fires.
'Cause tonight, my lips belong to you,
and [i] will place them…
on the coordinates that lead to your waterfall.
'Cause tonight, my tongue belongs to you,
and [i] perform surgery with the tip
making acupuncture a thing of the past.
[i] want to wake in the morning
with the taste of your cinnamon soul in my mouth.

See, the best time is when we wake up
in the middle of the night,
drifting along the sea of Blackness.
(Ain't nothing like that three a.m. loving.)
Eyes closed tighter than a snare drum,
nothing but the night's quilted comforter and us.
And we both know that this act
will lead to some hellified sleep.
For [i] still get that hump in my back,
and every time [i] straighten it out,
you hit those high notes that
only the dogs in the back yard can hear.
For every time we make love,
it's like doing it for the first time.
It's like the first time [i] saw the sun rise.
It's like the first time
[i] really got what [i] wanted for Christmas.

[i] remember when [i] used to pick
you up from work on your payday.
The first thing that you wanted to do
was pay your bills.

(That was so sexy to me.)
[i] remember when we wanted to see Roger and Zapp,
but your kids wanted to see Tupac.
So, you asked me to sacrifice our funds
so that they could be baptized in art.
(That was so sexy to me.)
And [i] remember the first time that you made me
smothered chicken, cabbages, cornbread,
yams, ice tea, and pecan pie.
(That was so sexy to me.)

Girl, your Psychedelica is so good that you make
all of my tomorrows an adventure yet to come
and everyday one long orgasm.
'Cause you still stimulate my nasty
'cause you still stimulate my soul.

Time Going

Where did its gypsy feet take it to?
Time strolls like a man with no job.
"Now [i] lay me down to sleep"
with innocence as my steel, shinning shield.
At twelve [i] tucked my ripe dreams under the covers,
and an alarm awakened me to withered prunes.
Time, never caring where the tornados land,
stares at me like a blank chalkboard.
Its eyes pass through me like a hot laser,
burning holes in my Swiss cheese soul.
[i]'m in a rocking chair on a porch
attached to nothing.

A vision of Black gold stands statue still on a hill top
protruding into a grassy knoll that rolls like a river.
Her hair of lamb's wool sways firmly in the spring breeze,
and she with her dangling long fingers beckons me
to follow autumn's swelling call.
But inside [i] know that she's loved this way before.

[i]'m not the nucleus of God's universe.
[i] revolve like a pitiful planet in my place
around Nature's selfish cycle.
My life not solid, liquid, or mist,
my footsteps are briefly etched upon the shifting sand.
The most that [i] can hope is that my fading paint
is a part of the swirling montage of the Everyman.
My life's an ambiguous allegory
with no dense denotation to me.
[i] can hear the robust Viking laughter of Determinism
as [i] pray to my God who's written me out of the
final chapter by the end of the first scene.

And Time is a master Parker Brother,
periodically blowing down the straw huts of my life.
Should [i] pray to Time?
[i] have nothing to sacrifice that He can't take.

But in an eye's twinkle,
the present is a rerun of my canceled past.
Yet, like blind students we pray for tomorrow's test
never finishing the homework of the day,
not understanding that the flowers of May
were not possible without April's rainy days.
And with just one kiss from Time, it's winter again.
So, we give up to fate and push our bolder
up life's hill sometimes for the sake of pushing.

Life Is a Parade

When everyday is a holyday,
and you cry with a smile,
and a trip around the universe
never exceeds a mile…
When the world is a rainbow quilt
that you wrap around you to smother
the cold breath of disappointment,
this is when your soul eats knowledge
that is as sweet as
chocolate chip cookies and strawberry lemonade
'cause for you my friend
life has become a parade.

Pre-Colonial

In my cold cage of colonialism,
being eating away by the rats and cancer of capitalism,
[i] wish [i] was a before the Mayflower African.
Freedom is wind that erodes the clay of the body
so that the spirit can whirl like a leaf in the breeze.
Freedom is an ocean that allows single-celled countries
to grow into a Nation of whales.
Only free people can cry themselves better.
Only free people can fall down and not detest the dirt.

Sometimes [i] wish that
[i] was warmed by Akhenaton's heat,
then [i] could see the Sun with no pasty film
and know that God is here with me
because the pounding pheromones of his thoughts
keep the time of my bleeding drum
from the DNA of the Aton which is the light of me,
knowing that the only limits
are those that [i] purchase with misspent knowledge.

Sometimes [i] wish that
[i] drank from Egypt's Mississippi
before it was dammed by Greek stones,
then [i] wouldn't suffer from the
continuous, clanging headaches
from thinking too much or not enough or not at all,
trying to figure out just where to place my feet
on a white carpeted land filled with
economic landmines and judicial tripwires
designed for my demise.

Sometimes [i] wish that
my notebooks were lined with papyrus
then [i] could hurl hieroglyphs to the high heavens
without worry that my words might
offend a kingly peon who's just looking
for a reason to banish me to the curse of Ham.
Then [i] could rock with my grandfather

a decade after his death,
and our laughter will rise like vapor
filling the clouds with our moist morphemes
then released back to us by the Son of the Most High
raining down tears of antiquarian seeds,
and [i] would eat of his flesh from fruit trees
and drink of his soul from cool, clear springs
remembering our communion on a daily basis.

[i] wanna throw my head back, show my pearly whites
and laugh so loudly that you can see my tonsils.
But [i] can't 'cause [i]'m cool.
"Cool," a box designed to cage people in their insecurities.
Don't talk too loudly and draw a crowd of
conservative cowards wanting to use your Black body
as silver payments into mas'sa's good graces.
Don't use words with blistering balm that awaken
sleeping warriors to battle.
Don't ask questions
that make man face his sickly sanctimoniousness.
Don't speak out of turn.
Wait patiently to be acknowledge at the back door
for the crumbs of life
recycled from the garbage of the citizens.

And [i], in my drunken stupor of integration, tow the line,
dancing to the rhythm of a drummer who hates me,
constantly building my own back door.

So sometimes, just sometimes,
[i] wish that [i] stood on the land
before Blackness was a badge of evil,
then [i] could sleep nude under the stars,
with the warm blanket of God's eyes
falling upon me.
And every Dawn would bring
a new day to fellowship in the Garden of Goodness.

Psychedelic World
(When we understand that human advancement is not the creation of things but the evolution of the soul, rejoining the plane of God)

When night and day can no longer bear their separation
and cling one to another, and the sun and the moon
form one orchid of fire against the Black sky
that vibrates like speakers, shaking the shimmering
stars that glitter on the sky's canvas into rewriting
our childhood constellations, setting His-story in its place.

This is when Dawn and Dusk mate and Forever is born.
When all the universe's inhabitants realize that the only
cure for the virus of Hate is the antibody of Love,
allowing rain to cascade down upon the glass
or our translucent bodies, washing us into new creatures.

Did you know that Love is merely energy that glows
as the eternal, every-ready battery of the universe
with a sonic shine, causing all under its umbrella
to appear as reversed film negatives with remnants
of streaking and pulsating colors manifesting itself
into thousands of prophets and doctrines, painting a path
of how to evolve back to it?

Midnight Black dirt (the richest of soil) speckled with pure white crystals is lying like a sleeping child under the aqua grass as nude souls play under the feet of God.
Rains fall for them; rivers flow for them.

When the only real color is that of emotion,
the sun flowing through droplets of rain
and all race is defined as God's…
When our technology serves to get us back to the Garden and our notion of advancement replaces what you can get with what you can give, we can then wash ourselves in the effulgence of his eyes.

When all you've ever been and all you'll ever be

converge like two locomotives at one point creating
the Big Bang of you,
making the epiphany a constant stream of consciousness
and the Sublime one eternal orgasm...
When the night is as bright as the day,
and the day is as calm as the night...

When Love becomes a democratic monarch,
and Hate is a far memory of a fallen tyranny...
When silk describes both the physical and the metaphysical
and the universe becomes one analogous plasma
of knowledge
creating an organic internet pathway for the brain
and all that we download are files of peace and cookies of
completion where fear is the snake that we've made a pet,
and we dance in individual harmony...

When birth-line is a lifeline
connecting us all back to the One,
and in full circle of the Genesis we have come,
realizing that from royalty is where we're all from, and Black is restored as the Father to the rainbow, this is when we know that from one ocean of humanity is from where each race of rivers flow, and uncertainty is just another opportunity to create.

good night...good morning...good morrow...
good life...good eternal...sweet dreams...

My Journey

If your silky hands ain't never picked cotton,
your opinion about me ain't worth dried excrement.
If you ain't never wrestled with dust devils in the cotton
fields, been blinded by the piercing bright saffron
of a hellish hot sun bouncing its evil glow
off shinny white cotton balls that
look like thousand watt light bulbs that
even when you close your eyes burn
bright as a noon day sun after a lynching…
So if your hollow hip-hop hands ain't never picked cotton,
your opinion is a car with no gas.
If you ain't never felt the pain of the rays like sharp,
stainless steel beating down across your back,
like a newly carved bullwhip leaving your soul scared with
the swelling welts of injustice,
the searing scabs of humiliation,
the pus-filled sores of degradation,
the ashy corns of oppression, and
the acid reflux of Jim Crow heartache,
and singing the blues is the only sedative you have
to keep from killing some mother's misguided son,
oh, [i] say from the Valley of the Delta
to the Midwest mountains,
if your Wall-Street paws ain't never picked cotton,
your opinion is a house with no roof.
If you ain't never wrapped your callus stained hands
around a dirty, splintered hoe,
like a prostitute wrapping her cracked lips
around a swollen rusted pipe
each chop just like each suck,
every slicing swing circumcising the skin layers of
your humanity, your dignity, your serenity, your sanity,
[i] say again,
if your plastic ivory tower palms ain't never picked cotton,
your opinion is a wristwatch with no hands.
If you ain't never felt the sting of hot thirst
like a ball of stickpins rolling down the back of your throat
and your fiery spit is too spicy to sooth your pain…

If you've ever tried to pry open your eyes
only to realize that your eyes were already open,
but you can't see for the foggy fumes of heat and sweat
popping, sizzling, and oozing out of your eyes,
like polluted rivers, and your equilibrium
is capsized like the Titanic so that walking humped over
feels better than standing up right,
oh [i] say for each salty boulder of sweat that
has fallen from my scarlet framed forehead
if your Jerry Springer drenched hands ain't never picked
cotton your opinion is like a school with no teachers
'cause a man who has picked cotton
can harvest the crops grown at any college
because the buildings, the programs, and the faculty
were fertilized within the soil that he tilled.
A man who has picked cotton
can cash an unemployment check without an
albatross of guilt hanging around his broken-down psyche.
A man who has picked cotton
can sit on the bus where he wants to sit
eat in the Woolworth's where he wants to eat
can sleep in the hotel where he wants to sleep
can dance in the Ritz where he wants to dance
and can pollinate whom he wants to pollinate.
So if your 1st and the 15th outstretched palms
ain't never picked cotton,
your opinion is two left shoes tryin' to make a right turn.

II

So, spit out like swine the New York and L.A. naysayers
and their pseudo-psycho revolutionary writers.
Flush down the toilets of your minds
the golden gatekeepers of
Random House, Ballatine, and St. Martin's Press.
[i]'m so glad [i] got my insanity in time.
[i]'m so glad [i] got my insanity in time.
Singing gloriofunkdofantabulos
[i] got my insanity in time
'cause insanity will sit-in and take lashes to free me.

For slavery is when you surrender yourself
to the narcotic of normality.
Slavery is when we join organizations because
we are too fragile to face the winds of the world alone.
Slavery is when the Sweet-n-Low Splenda of Religion
is substituted for the sugarcane of spirituality.
Slavery is when [i] exchange
the tailor-made threads of individuality
for the traditional in-style overcoat of acceptance.
Slavery is marriage bound by
the wedding-band of financial convenience.
Slavery is buying a new car to get new friends,
while drowning in the quicksand of your old bills.
Slavery is the illusion of integration formed by
the smoking mirrors of legal change and the successful
mirage of the Brown vs. the Board of Education
as Ayers is an alarm clock to our nightmare.
Slavery is the fear of Black Nationalism painted by the
10:00 o'clock news' creation of the Negro Boogieman.

III

Free the slave! Say what you just wanna say!
Free the slave! Say what you just wanna say!
The language is yours! Say what you just wanna say!
Man is not concubine to the language!
Say what you just wanna say!
Language is a hammer to be wielded by man!
Say what you just wanna say!
It's time to break the chains that hopelessly tie us
to the bureaucratic monster which is society.
The only good fruit grown by society is taxes,
but we spoil and squander it away on the maggots of more
bureaucracy instead of investing in the forest of education.
But that'll never happen because an investment in
public education is an investment in the
green germination of individuals,
and the last thing that this mindless mesh of weeds wants
are more budding individuals.
We've got to break the ferocious chains of fear and free

the children willing to run toward the sun rather than
allowing ourselves to be pimped by panic and phobia.
[i] will not be imprisoned by a paycheck.
[i] will not be high-jacked by a car note.
[i] will not be held hostage by the rent.
[i] will not be enslaved by the light bill.
[i] will not be straight-jacketed by student loans.
Even if these bills explode like bombs and
blow over my straw hut life,
[i] will still swim against the stream of social slavery.
[i] will not be chained by snake slick social acceptance.
[i] will not be chained by the pneumonia of anxiety.
[i] will not be chained by
glittering gold-painted glass posing as love.
Love is not an oppressive landlord.
Love opens the birdcage for you to fly free.
So if someone who loves you
tries to chain you—bound and gag you,
that mutha-hubba pit-bull punk don't love you
'cause Love is free.
[i] will not be chained by the cement shoes of ignorance.
[i] will not be chained by hate because hating you creates
holes in my heart that drains like sand my energy for life
so [i] blow you off with a wink and a "fuck you,"
hopscotch and leapfrog over you, and continue
painting the portraits for my tomorrow's landscape.
James, hit me three times.
[i] will not be, [i] will not be, [i] will not be chained.

IV

So, to all of the Hellacious Haters who ask me
"C. Liegh, with all of your neon profanity,
with all of your back-alley vulgarity, with all of your
chittlin' bucket insanity, what kind of motivational message
could you possibly have for wooly-haired children?"
My message is as simple as scrambling eggs.
Successful people identify the silver knobs and
stroll through the doors of opportunity.
Great people construct golden archways of opportunity

then hang lights for the rest to be lead from darkness.
So, when in the midst of your journey to greatness
and someone puts a heavy, immovable white wall
in your path to stop your progress,
take your steel shoes weighted with the
steps of Sojourner and the stomps of Sammy and
kick a crumbling hole in their cheap sheetrock,
and that'll become your doorway to success.

www.ingramcontent.com/pod-product-compliance
Lightning Source LLC
Chambersburg PA
CBHW032148040426
42449CB00005B/440